Found My Heart When I Lost My Way

By: Bruce Pittman

Dedication
"My Four Heroes"

Have you ever moved from a place you loved? It is heartbreaking isn't it? The friendships, laughter and fun times you shared with people are difficult to release. My family knows that very well. In the spring of 2001, we left behind great friends to plant a new church. It was life changing for all of us. I still remember when we told our sons that we felt like GOD was calling us elsewhere. While they were not happy about the move, they were willing to go with us. (What else could they do right?) And together we stepped into a new season of life. And together we started a new church.

As I think about the people who deserve the most credit for this book and the story behind it, four individuals come to mind. They are my four heroes. The first person is my amazing wife, Kim. She had no idea that she was marrying a dreamer in 1984. Neither did she know what it meant. Her support has been my lifeline on so many days. While words cannot express the depth of my gratitude, still I try, "Kim, Thank You!"

Two other individuals that I would call my heroes are my sons, Ryan and Wesley. I think that they paid the highest price of this whole journey. They left a network of friends and security to walk into the great unknown following their dad and mom. They have taught me as much as I have taught them. "Ryan and Wesley - You guys rock! Thanks for helping me become the dad I needed to be."

The last hero is the greatest. It's Jesus. Far, far above everyone else there He stands. He invited me to this journey out of His deep love for me. While there were many days I did not understand that, I look back now and see it all more clearly. Though there have been people more willing than me, still Jesus has patiently called me day by day to follow Him down unknown roads and into fearful places. He has been inviting me to more. What can I say in response to love so astonishing and grace so compelling?

Now to the King eternal, immortal, invisible,
the only GOD,
be honor and glory forever and ever. Amen.
1 Timothy 1:17

A Word of Gratitude

Several people have read this manuscript and I am grateful for those who were willing to read it and offer feedback. Special thanks go to Melodie Holton and Randall W. Harrell. I am very grateful for your corrections and thoughtful suggestions. The time you invested was huge.

Bruce Pittman
December 2013

Acknowledgements

VOICE OF TRUTH
**Written by: Steven Curtis Chapman & John Mark
Hall**
© 2003 Sony/ATV Music Publishing LLC, My Refuge
Music and Sparrow Song. All rights on behalf of
Sony/ATV Music Publishing LLC administered by
Sony/ATV Music Publishing LLC, 8 Music Square
West, Nashville, TN 37203. All rights reserved. Used by
permission.

Table of Contents

Introduction

Have you ever been lost? I have. Twice.

I was lost before I followed Jesus. And then I got lost after I followed Jesus. I did not know where to go or what to do. I woke up one morning and the footprints I had been following for decades just disappeared. Right out of sight. And I was lost.

If you are reading this, perhaps you know what I mean. You don't know which way to turn. No open doors await you. Should you go left or right? Should you turn around? No direction is certain. It is all vague. That was me – lost. And this is my story.

Prayer of Thomas Merton[i]

MY LORD GOD, I have no idea where I am going.
I do not see the road ahead of me.
I cannot know for certain where it will end.
Nor do I really know myself,
And the fact that I think I am following Your will does not mean that I am actually doing so.
But I believe that the desire to please You does in fact please You.
And I hope I have that desire in all that I am doing.
I hope that I will never do anything apart from that desire.
And I know that if I do this You will lead me by the right road,
Though I may know nothing about it.
Therefore I will trust You
Always though I may seem to be lost
And in the shadow of death.
I will not fear, for You are ever with me,
And You will never leave me to face my perils alone.

No One Ever Told Me

The spiritual life is characterized by movement and discovery, challenge and change, adversity and joy, uncertainty and fulfillment.
It is also marked in a special way by companionship, first with the One we seek to follow and second with those who also seek to follow Jesus Christ.[ii]

No one ever told me that following Jesus could get me lost, especially this far along in the journey. I was raised by Christian parents so following Jesus was a part of my upbringing. I understood the word picture of following Him very well. It meant the road before me would always have footprints in them and He would direct my life. I always thought that my obedience would be the problem, not His direction. I was told that He would always have a destination.

And that is the way it had been for many years. Generally, I had known which paths to take. If not, clarity was rarely far away. I knew the relationship with my fiancé was headed to a marriage altar, I knew that marriage meant having children, I knew my next step after college was theological training and I knew that graduation meant pastoring a church. As I look back on my life, I see that a clear path was marked for me. The Holy Spirit had always shown me the direction He wanted me to travel. I led my family by that mooring. I led churches by that same philosophy. The next step of GOD'S plan was always clear. Disorientation for a Christ Follower was a foreign thought to me until I did not know what the next step was or where it was headed.

Where Was He?

My faith was shrouded by darkness and confusion. My heart cried out to GOD for guidance because I longed to follow Him. I prayed and fasted for direction. I did not know where to go. I did not know what to do. I found myself second guessing my decisions. I felt the heaviness of GOD'S distance and silence. My mind was filled with questions and doubts. Where was He? Where was I? And why? Why was I lost now? What happened to those footprints in the sand?

This confusing season started when I planted a church five years earlier. Church planting had been a tremendous time, but it had also been a challenging time. I knew that the start-up of a church was out of my skill set, but I could not get away from the sense of calling from GOD. So I left a decade of joyful ministry at a caring church to do something new. It was a decision two years in the making for my wife and me. We knew it was the right thing to do. We saw His footprints ahead of us so we followed. My family and I gave our hearts and souls to the work for five years. The struggle was great on us. We gave away our lives and came to a point where we had nothing else to give. I began to feel like my lack of energy was hindering the church. They deserved more than what I was giving. So did my family.

One specific evening is memorable. We had put together a prayer experience that very few attended. The planning and preparation left us exhausted. After it was over, my wife, Kim, and I were alone at the church building cleaning up. We had stopped to eat and she prayed, "Lord, we need You to move and to move quickly." In that prayer, we felt a confirmation in our hearts that it was the end for us there. With the support of my family, I resigned.

It sounds like burnout. And it was. Yet it was more. I have read the stories of several church planters who burned out, but after a sabbatical season, they returned and the church continued to prosper. But I could not return. Even after the church granted me an extended leave of absence, nothing in my soul even leaned towards returning to the church plant. I believe that was GOD leading me away from that work. I saw His footprints even though I did not really understand why He was taking me a different direction. They were not clear, but they were evident. As best I knew, I was following Him away from the community and church to which He had brought me.

No Open Door

Then it happened. I woke up dark, confused and disoriented. I had no idea where to go or what to do next. Jesus' footprints were not evident anymore. It was a terrible place to be. So I began searching for a job, any job to take care of my family. I looked for almost a year before I found employment. I also inquired about different pastoring opportunities, but to no avail. I sent out hundreds of resumes and nothing opened up.

Finances were more than tight. They were strangling us. We were barely breathing, and yet GOD was faithfully providing. We paid our mortgage, had food on the table, kept gas in our cars and were still able to keep our children in a private school. One of the means by which GOD provided for their education was through financial aid that the school offered. We applied for financial aid for the next year. The company that assesses these applications denied us aid because they said our income was too low to provide any type of contribution on our part. Yet the school was willing to risk with us that GOD would provide the funds. He did. Along with other numerous personal challenges facing us, my wife had multiple medical issues that took more than a year to resolve. It seemed as if our world was caving in.

The old saying about closed doors leading to open doors was not proving to be true for me. A door had closed, but no new doors had opened. During this time, my prayers were marked with question marks. "GOD, what is going on? Why do no churches want me? Why can't I even find a job?" I felt like a failure. Was GOD disciplining me? Had I disqualified myself from ministry? Was this burnout the last straw? Maybe GOD did not have a place on His team for me. These questions became louder to me as I heard of other guys who seemed to find churches to pastor at will. It was like they had a choice of where they wanted to go. Was I that bad a pastor? I did not think so. Many days I wondered if I would ever return to a place of leadership. The negative voices were strong during that time. I really did feel lost.

After a year, I was grateful to find a job as a Bereavement Coordinator at a local hospice. While counseling people in grief was not something I desired to do, I found it was quite rewarding. GOD used me to help people who were deeply hurting and questioning Him much like I was. Although I could not always relate to losing a loved one, I could relate to loss because I had lost my job, my career, a church family, my calling and a web of relationships. I would feel a heavy sadness whenever I would think of the church plant. That church was the fruition of a dream that was lodged deeply in my heart and now it was gone. I remember crying on my drive to work on several occasions. Very little about this season of life was anything I wanted.

I had spent the majority of my life trying to follow Jesus. Not that I had always followed Him. Frequently I had made decisions that were not what He desired. Yet repentance always drew my heart back to Him because I knew that was the only life worth living. However, it seemed that Jesus was no longer interested in leading me.

What Kind of Friend Doesn't Respond?

I felt as if I was pursuing an ever-elusive lover. This pursuit of GOD reminded me of the guy who finally finds the woman of his dreams. His heart is smitten with her beauty. He does everything to woo her to himself, only to find that she spurns his every effort. Regardless of his attempts to win her heart, she refuses him. Why did GOD keep me at a distance? Why was He aloof?

Seth Barnes described this season of life in his book, *Kingdom Journeys.* He found himself in a similar situation after starting a new ministry, describing it as a "dark phase."

Somewhere in that desperate place, I cried out to GOD. All I seemed to get in response was silence. It confirmed what I'd always suspected, but was only coming to believe: we Christians could advertise a "personal relationship with Jesus Christ" until we were blue in the face, but whatever relationship I had with GOD was decidedly impersonal. What kind of friend doesn't respond when you call on them?[iii]

I felt his pain. The silence was deafening and unnerving. I was lost and wondering what to do. Nothing seemed to make sense.

This season did not last just a few months. Instead it lasted for years. I had heard of others living with uncertainty for a short time, but never for this long. My heart toward GOD grew cold. My wife expressed it like this: "If He does not want to talk to us, then why should we bother Him? GOD knows we are here when He gets ready to talk." The songs of worship I had sung with great pleasure at one time faded. My relationship with GOD had gone from a Father-son relationship to a Boss-worker relationship. The only problem is that my Boss had nothing to say to me and my efforts to restore my love for Him diminished.

No one ever told me that following Jesus could get you lost. But it happened to me. GOD is always clear isn't He? Maybe not.

Discussion Questions

1. Henry Blackaby wrote about a "Crisis of Faith" in *Experiencing GOD.* Describe a season in your life when you were in such a crisis. Have you ever felt lost while following Jesus?

2. Were you surprised by this time in life? Why or why not?

3. Describe the emotions you felt during this time.

4. What/who helped you deal with this crisis the most?

5. Discuss Thomas Merton's prayer.

A GOD Moment
Bruce Pittman

Waiting, waiting
    Looking and listening,
A phone call, an email
    Some kind of sign that I am in the process,
That God is at work –
    Behind the scenes,
    In the dark.

Isn't that place – the dark –
    Where God does His best work?
    A growing fetus,
    A planted seed,
    A dead Jesus.

But nothing . . . only silence.

Where is the dilation for birth?
Where is the rain to water the soil?
Where is the angel to move the stone?

I don't need an answer.
    I need to know that behind the emptiness of this
season
        There is a purpose being fulfilled,
        A plan being accomplished.

Where there's a plan, there's hope
    That this is just a season.
        It awakens a deeper faith
            That can trust God for one more day.

GOD Confusing Me?

The church planting experience included seasons when things were moving forward and doing well. We grew in the number of attenders. Our offerings even flourished. It was at one particular finance meeting during this thriving time that I asked the finance team about giving away 10% of our offerings. "What do you think? Should we do it?" I asked. Around the room, the Finance Team agreed that we should take the plunge. Our offerings had exceeded our needs by a large amount. We felt it was time to give more away than we ever had. We had wanted to give away 10% of our offerings before and now we could finally do that. So we did. Our Treasurer wrote the check that week and we felt as if we were finally making progress financially. We also felt like we were honoring GOD by our giving. The Bible encourages us to give generously even when we do not have an abundance, so we stepped out in faith believing that as we gave away, GOD would provide and replenish. It was a moment of success for us.

Then came the rest of the Sundays in the month. The offerings were not so good. In fact, they were actually bad. They were so bad that for the first time, we could not pay our building rent. They were so bad that I could not even get my full salary.

"Wait! What just happened?" was my question. Our leadership had just decided to step out in faith by giving away 10% of our offerings and as a result, our needs were not met. Faith is not supposed to work like that. Faith leads to success not failure. Shouldn't GOD be meeting all of our needs? Even Jesus had said that our giving would return to us, *"good measure, pressed down, shaken together and running over"* (Luke 6:38).

Well, not meaning to be irreverent, but calling the landlord to say we could not pay all of our rent just proved all of that wrong. It was like GOD has thrown us under the bus. I did not understand this at all. I was confused.

When GOD is Unclear

Uncertainty is a pattern we see throughout the Bible. GOD'S plan for His leaders always took them through seasons of disorientation where they experienced loss. The result was that they were able to gain a new and better future.

For instance, Joseph, an Old Testament character, had a season of disorientation. He had a dream of being a powerful leader. It was GOD'S dream for him as well, but it was not in the manner that Joseph had thought it would happen. He never thought the path to becoming a world leader would take him through slavery and imprisonment, but GOD led Joseph through a seventeen-year period that would disorient his thinking and prepare him to rescue Egypt and the people of Israel from starvation. In the end, his dreams were fulfilled. He not only became a world leader, but he also was eventually reunited with his estranged family, including his father. The words of Genesis 46:29 describe the touching moment when Joseph and Jacob were reunited: *"As soon as Joseph appeared before him, he threw his arms around his father and wept for a long time."* Both had longed for this moment for many years. Jacob had given up the chance of ever seeing his son again, yet GOD granted them the desires of their hearts.

Moses experienced this kind of disorientation as a shepherd in Midian. At one time, he had a desire to set the Israelite slaves free in Egypt through a revolution. In Acts 7, Stephen retold this story:

"When Moses was forty years old, he decided to visit his own people, the Israelites. He saw one of them being mistreated by an Egyptian, so he went to his defense and avenged him by killing the Egyptian. Moses thought that his own people would realize that GOD was using him to rescue them, but they did not."

It was GOD'S dream for Moses to lead them to freedom as well, but not through a bloody revolution. It would take another forty years before GOD would use Moses to liberate the Israelite slaves from Egypt. Moses had to be reshaped before GOD could use Him to accomplish His plan. After ten miraculous plagues and the parting of the Red Sea, the Israelites were set free and Pharaoh's army was destroyed without the loss of a single Israelite life. The way that Moses thought about GOD'S ways had to be changed. GOD gave him a time of disorientation to remodel his thinking.

The twelve apostles of Jesus experienced a time of disorientation when they started following Jesus. They had been brought up in the Jewish way of life. They believed along with everyone else that GOD would eventually send a Messiah to save Israel. Little did they know that Jesus was the one. However, when they took to the road with Jesus, their understanding of GOD was radically disoriented. Much of what He said and did made little sense to them. On several occasions Jesus asked them if they understood because they obviously did not. His parables and lessons often left them scratching their heads. Their disorientation was no greater than it was when He died like a criminal on the cross. On the near side of His death, they were confused and afraid. They went and hid. However, on the other side of that tragedy, the puzzle pieces created a beautiful picture and it made sense. Once reoriented, they went out and changed the world. We see this disorienting pattern of GOD repeated throughout the scriptures.

Lonnie's Move to Lynch

Lonnie Riley is an individual who learned this lesson of walking by faith. In 1999, he and his wife moved to Lynch, Kentucky, to start Meridzo Center Ministries. It is a ministry geared toward the impoverished residents of Lynch and the surrounding area. He left a growing church and moved to no church. GOD was calling him to a life of greater faith. He reminds us of how GOD worked in the Bible:

"Typically, when GOD began leading people in Scripture, He led them into the unknown. He required changes in their belief system, habits, role, or character. Most received assignments they could never live up to on their own. Do you think Moses had any inkling what lay before him when GOD called him at the burning bush? He would become a deliverer, an administrator, an intercessor, a lawgiver and a nation builder. He went from doubt about his speaking abilities at the burning bush to trusting GOD to split the Red Sea. GOD began to transform him as he trusted Him by faith with a teachable spirit. The unknown requires that we continue relying on GOD throughout the process with that same teachable spirit. Interestingly, GOD did not grant skills or great faith to Moses at his call. GOD gave these attributes to Moses as he obeyed. Moses did not wait until

*he was qualified; rather, GOD qualified him in the
process of his obedience."[iv]*

Once I saw that disorientation was one of GOD'S ways,
I had a new appreciation for my lostness. These kinds
of seasons were not out of the ordinary for people of
faith. In fact, they were more common than I realized.

Adversity Has An Upside

The story of Os Hillman was a great encouragement
to me. His book, *The Upside of Adversity*, chronicles
his experiences and lessons from a disorienting season
of life. Hillman was a very wealthy Christ Follower
who lost his business and family in a matter of a few
months. It was devastating to him. He too felt the
silence and absence of heaven. None of it made sense.
His experience that he describes as a "Joseph Pit" lasted
seven years. As Hillman reflected on that season of life,
he wrote:

*Sometimes GOD has to take us into the desert in order
to get Egypt out of our system. We have to experience a
separation from our old lives in order to receive the new
one that GOD has planned for us.[v]*

He understood the greater purposes of his Heavenly
Father. Today Hillman is leader of a global workplace
ministry equipping Christ Followers to live out their
faith at their jobs. More than 250,000 people receive his
daily email of encouragement. GOD took him to a new
place, not just externally but internally as well. GOD
had to radically reorient him from the inside out. And
today he is a world changer. His life has become much
more than he could have ever imagined.

Hillman's words helped me tremendously because they relieved many of my fears. GOD was accomplishing His plans during this season of disorientation, which meant that GOD had not given up on me. He had not sidelined me permanently. Instead, a new future awaited me. However, that new future required a new me. I could not become what I needed to become with the old me. Not only was GOD disorienting me, He was also reorienting me. He was changing me drastically from the inside. I had a restored confidence that He would see me through this time. GOD was not trying to destroy me. Instead, He was trying to remake me for His divine plans.

On many days during this darkness I would reflect on the way things used to be and I would wish for those days when life was more settled and certain, those days when I knew where I was going and what I was doing. One morning as I read the story of Joseph in Genesis 39, I saw how GOD had given him success in all areas of his life. And I thought to myself, "If Joseph had not been sold as a slave to Egypt and had stayed in Canaan, He would have been just as successful there at home. As a result, his brothers would have reacted out of jealousy and would have eventually killed him. Their terrible act of betrayal actually saved his life." And I realized then that the struggles we were facing actually were the best thing that could have occurred to us. Without them, I shudder to consider where I would be today and how much less the future would hold.

Following Jesus is not always a clear path like we think it should be. GOD often takes us to places where questions make up our prayers. However, like an architect overseeing a remodeling project, GOD knows what we must lose in order to give us what we need so we can become what He desires.

Discussion Questions

1. Have you ever faced a moment of failure like the church plant did with its offerings?

How do you respond when your faith appears to have failed?

2. Discuss your thoughts regarding this statement:

"GOD knows what we must lose in order to give us what we need so we can become what He desires."

3. Lonnie Riley in his book, *By Faith*, states:

"Teachability is an attitude that rejects the clamoring voices of fear insisting that we return to our comfort zone."

When your faith has led you through darkness, have you maintained a spirit of teachability?

If so, how? If not, how has fear kept you from growing while in the darkness?

The God of Just Enough
Bruce Pittman

Like manna from heaven has come daily provision,
Just enough for today, just enough.
The rent is soon due and one offering on Sunday,
Will it be enough? Just enough?
The kids are thirsty. They want more of You.
Will someone step up soon?
Will a volunteer be enough? Just enough?

Where is the God of glorious riches?
Where are the cattle on a thousand hills?
Where is the God who rewards sacrifice and faith?
Are You the God of Just Enough?
You who keep us barely alive,
You who sustain us as we look for the
breakthrough that will never come.

And yet this I remember –
It is Your work. I am Your servant.
My responsibility is faithfulness,
Your responsibility is success.
So I will trust Your heart for me,
And for me right now – Just enough is enough.

Dealing with the Disappointment

I have rarely struggled with trusting GOD. My challenge has always been that I seemed to trust Him for too much. Reading the stories in the Bible has led me to think that nothing was too big for GOD. Those events were phenomenal experiences. When I read of David's fight against a nine-foot Goliath or of the Red Sea splitting and a million people walking through it or of Lazarus hopping out of a tomb, then my thoughts led me to believe that GOD could do anything. If He could suspend the laws of the entire universe to work for the sake of His servants, then He could do anything for me. The dreamer in me has usually risen to the occasion and seen the possibilities of what GOD could do rather than the obstacles that would hinder GOD. It seems that I have often expected too much of GOD.

That is why I was not afraid to step into the world of church planting. Taking that step was the result of a lengthy process. My wife and I had felt for two years like GOD was leading us to a new place of service, but we were unsure where or what. We had asked trusted friends for input. We had continuously prayed for guidance and had continuously read the Scriptures. We listened to people like Henry Blackaby, author of *Experiencing GOD*, for clarity. At the end of our search was a calling to move to our hometown to plant a church, one that would be non-traditional and geared toward reaching people who were not actively involved in a church.

However, we also knew that we were not the church planting types either. Church planters are a different breed of leaders (and I mean that in a good way). Most of them are entrepreneurial, out of the box, catalytic, by the seat of their pants world changers. A church planting friend described himself and other planters as "guys who may not know what they are doing, but they do it with a lot of passion." So I knew that planting would be outside of the structured ministry mindset that I had practiced for years.

The other challenge was that we were planting a church in an area where many churches already existed and where a new church had not been successfully started in a very long time. Even though the population was at least 70% unchurched, very few thought a new church was needed. But we did, so I left a wonderful church to go out on my own and start something that I believed would connect with unchurched people.

The Great Faithfulness of GOD

With those two challenges looming on the horizon, I knew that if this church were to get off the ground, it may require GOD to step up and suspend the universe on my behalf, if necessary. I was convinced that it was beyond me. Like Moses and David and Lazarus, this situation would require supernatural power. And that is one reason I wanted to do it. I wanted others to see the great faithfulness of GOD as He directed this new work and provided all the resources that would be required to start this work. I was not concerned that people see what I could do, but rather what GOD could do through someone willing to risk everything for the sake of His Kingdom.

I also wanted my sons to see the faithfulness of GOD firsthand. The church I was serving at the time was a missions minded church. Our sons had read about and prayed for missionaries all of their lives. They had read the stories of people in the Bible and from history who had stepped out and trusted GOD to provide for them as they walked in the realm of utter dependence on Him. I wanted our children to know this way of life from their own experience. I wanted them to have personal stories of how they had a GOD-sized need. They prayed and GOD met their need. Prayer was our method of operating. We had to trust Him for everything and He came through in a big way. Our move was filled with awe-inspiring moments of GOD's provision. Before moving, the four of us got together and compiled a prayer list of specific things. Every one of those requests was met. We asked specifically and we received specifically. Our depth of gratitude went to another level because we saw Him doing things in response to our simple prayers. We were experiencing GOD.

Great Risks for Greater Success

And yet the move involved a cost for us and the cost was significant. We moved away from great friends, an incredible church family, financial security, and successful ministry. They were people we had grown to value highly during the previous decade. We were giving up everything in order to do this one thing. For us it was a great sacrifice.

That is why we believed that this new church would take off. We were giving everything we had for it and it was requiring a lot of GOD to make it happen. As I read the Scriptures, those two things seem to be involved in every great work of GOD. Moses was ill-equipped to lead the people out of Egypt and he risked everything to do so. Simon Peter had no leadership skills and yet he risked everything to follow Jesus and ultimately lead the church.

I had also read of this combination in great movements of GOD from history. People who risked everything in situations that required much from GOD were recipes for great success. So we took the leap into the chasm of GOD'S faithfulness to start a church oriented toward reaching a new generation of believers for the honor of GOD. I was filled with great expectations.

I knew that this adventure was about more than the start-up of a church. I knew that GOD was interested in doing a deep and significant work in our lives. While we were excited that He had great plans for us, we look back now and realize that we knew nothing about the greater plans on His mind. We were confident that He was doing something big, but were totally unaware of how big or what it would look like.

A Steep, Uphill Climb

The truth that I learned to live with every day was that while GOD can do everything, He may not. The first couple of years were filled with wonder and astonishment. We saw some great things happen. As time progressed, the work became an uphill climb and it seemed to get steeper and steeper. Yet the church grew from our family of four to a crowd of more than a hundred in about five years. It took longer than we anticipated and it took more than we expected. We became weary in the work. We found that we were investing ourselves in many people who needed us emotionally and spiritually, but that we had very few investing in us. The stress that came with no structure and little financial support took its toll on us. We were running on empty during the months that led up to my resignation. We were simply getting by. I felt that my lack of energy was a hindrance to the church. I believed someone else could come in with energy and lead the work further.

We walked away feeling disappointed. After all I had given and after all I had read of GOD, how is it that something that seemed so awesome on the front-end turned out to be such a disaster in the end? I had expected more and ended up with less, much less. I had believed Him to do immeasurably more than I could imagine. I had given myself for Him to do just that. I had cut every cord but the one attached to His call and purpose. And where had that gotten me? To a place called nowhere and with nothing to show for it. I had expectations of GOD. He did not meet those expectations. I was disappointed.

The disappointment only continued. Now that I was free from the church, surely an established church would call. After all, I had nineteen years of experience and two graduate degrees. Just as GOD had directed us to plant this church, we believed He would direct us into a new future. So we waited for that path to become clear. While a couple of opportunities came our way, they simply did not feel like GOD'S leading. So we continued to wait. And we waited. And we waited.

And once again, we were disappointed. No direction came from heaven. No road was clear. Nothing was beckoning. We were in the wilderness of limbo. Silence was the noise we heard. It lasted not for days or weeks or months. It lasted for years.

Voice of Truth

One of the songs I heard regularly on the radio during that time was *Voice of Truth* by the group, Casting Crowns. Here are the lyrics:

Oh what I would do to have
The kind of faith it takes
To climb out of this boat I'm in
On to the crashing waves
To step out of my comfort zone
Into the realm of the unknown
Where Jesus is
And He's holding out His hand

But the waves are calling out my name
And they laugh at me
Reminding me of all the times
I've tried before and failed
The waves they keep on telling me
Time and time again
"Boy, you'll never win!
You'll never win!"

Oh what I would do to have
The kind of strength it takes to stand before a giant
With just a sling and a stone
Surrounded by the sound of a thousand warriors
Shaking in their armor
Wishing they'd have had the strength to stand

But the giant's calling out my name and he laughs
*   at me*
Reminding me of all the times I've tried before and
*   failed*
The giant keeps on telling me
Time and time again "boy, you'll never win!
"You'll never win"

But the voice of truth tells me a different story
The voice of truth says, "Do not be afraid!"

And the voice of truth says, "This is for My glory"
Out of all the voices calling out to me
I would choose to listen and believe the voice of
truth[vi]

As the song played, I would cry out, "GOD, I did that. I did just that. I stepped out of the security of the boat and onto the stormy waves. I went against the giant and I lost GOD! I lost! I did everything right and look at where I am now! I trusted You would make this new church an amazing display of Your wisdom and power, but look at it now Lord. It is nothing now. Nothing!" My heart was broken. I felt I had taken the steps of faith that would surely lead to success and it only led to being lost and forgotten.

The voice of truth was very quiet during this time while the voices of the waves and the giants were loud. I battled negative thoughts like never before in my entire life. I have always been a positive person. I have always seen the half-full glass. While I maintained a generally optimistic attitude during this time, I was fighting a battle against negativity and discouragement.

Battling the Voices

This battle was new territory for me and it was huge. I learned to never discount the powerful influence that negative voices can have on a heart. Those voices can be overwhelming. They steal energy and suffocate passion. They can destroy a life. At first, I did not know what to do with them so I embraced them. I walked in the valleys of depression. I allowed the darkness to envelope my soul. And though I practiced the spiritual disciplines that encourage weary souls, nothing changed. I read scripture regularly and prayed and worshipped and fasted and shared life with others, but the voices of the giants and waves kept calling me out and attempted to impose a new name on me.

Gradually, I began to recognize them for what they were, and I realized that I had to fight against them. I could not just succumb to the pressure and take on their new identity for me. I could not allow them to control my thinking and my emotions. I had to refuse them entrance into my mind. I learned to recognize when my thoughts would begin a downward spiral and when I did, I learned not to go there. I learned to think different thoughts and to overcome the negative voices.

The Bible was a huge help to me once I learned that the giants and waves were shouting to me. My journal records several experiences of reading the Bible that were meaningful. I recall on a morning run that the words of James 1:4 came to me. It reads: *"Perseverance must finish its work that you may be mature and complete, not lacking anything."* I was so encouraged to know that GOD was giving me sustaining strength that was enabling me to press on and that a finish line was in my future. My goal became to simply finish. I had no other prayer or desire. I wanted to make this happen and to gain the persevering heart that GOD wanted to give to me.

Disappointed with Jesus

Little did I know that the new path GOD was calling me to travel was not a new location. Rather it was a new work He desired to do inside of me. The church plant was a huge challenge like nothing I had ever done. And it wiped me out. However this new path was even beyond that. It was much greater. It was a radical disorienting season of life where nothing seemed to make sense. All I knew was the sufficiency of GOD that enabled me to survive. Prior to this moment in life, following Jesus meant a specific direction and path. But now, nothing was clear. It was all disorienting. I was unsure of everything. I questioned all my decisions from the previous years many times. Should I have moved and planted? Should I have resigned? Should I have gone back? What did I do wrong? Had GOD put me on the shelf? Was He finished with me? I spent many days trying to discern what all this meant. And at the end of those days, nothing was clearer. It was plain confusion. I had followed Jesus and was lost. How could that be?

When I looked at the Bible, I discovered that disappointment was nothing new for Christ Followers. As often as GOD answered the prayers of people, I also read that He delayed His answers to them or simply declined to answer them at all. How many years did the Israelites cry out to GOD during their enslavement in Egypt? They lived in the oppression for 400 years. The Old Testament tells of numerous times that the enemy invaded the Promised Land and GOD did not stop them. We read numerous stories in the Gospels where Jesus healed people. And we also read of people He did not heal. For instance, we read of a situation where Jesus met an invalid at a place where a number of sick people stayed. And He only healed the one guy. It leaves me asking the question: With all due respect Lord, did You not see the others who were sick? In Hebrews 11:36-38, Jesus' early followers were described:

> *"Some faced jeers and flogging, and even chains and imprisonment. They were put to death by stoning; they were sawed in two; they were killed by the sword. They went about in sheepskins and*

goatskins, destitute, persecuted and mistreated – the world was not worthy of them. They wandered in deserts and mountains, living in caves and in holes in the ground."

They hoped for something better in this life, but the something better did not happen. Later on we read that *"None of them received what had been promised."* GOD did not do as they asked. They suffered terribly as followers of Jesus. That statement is still true for thousands of believers around the globe. Disappointment was a part of their following Jesus. It was now a part of my following Him too.

Discussion Questions

1. What are some disappointments you have faced with GOD?

2. How long ago were they? Do they still linger in your heart today?

How did you respond?

3. Larry Crabb, *Shattered Dreams*, wrote:

> *"The farther we travel on our spiritual journey;*
> *the less responsive GOD becomes to our*
> *requests for a pleasant life."*

Have you found that to be true? If so, why do you think this statement is true?

4. How do you deal with negative voices that discourage you?

5. What have you found to be the biggest challenge during times of "just enough?"

Radical Re-Do

*"It is always our own self that we find at
the end of the journey.
The sooner we face that self, the better."*
Ella Maillart[vii]

We remodeled our kitchen many years ago. As with most do-it-yourself projects, it took longer than we anticipated, and the process did not happen as we thought. Remodeling the kitchen meant that everything in our house was affected. We had to eat at the dining room table for every meal instead of the kitchen table. We ordered new countertops to replace the old ones so we had to do without any counters for several weeks. As a result, we placed the microwave in the playroom where we also prepared the children's school lunches. It was chaotic to say the least. Everything was turned upside down. Our home was disoriented. Until we finished the project, nothing made sense. Our dishes were on the floor of the hallway. A bottle of syrup was on the toy box. The kitchen sink was in the carport. A person walking into this situation blindly would be confused. You could feel the disorder because nothing was as it should have been.

In my darkness, I was unaware that GOD was remodeling my life. None of it made sense. He was taking some things out and changing some things around because He had a different future planned for me than I understood. I was grieving all that I had lost and was losing, failing to recognize that those losses were necessary. However, GOD knew what I must lose in order to give me what I needed so I could become what He desired. Our kitchen project included a new dishwasher. In order for us to install that, we had to lose cabinet space. We had to adjust where we put some of our dishes and we had to find a new place for them. We happily did that because we would no longer need to wash dishes by hand. The future we had planned was better than the present in which we were living. Getting there required that we create a temporary chaos.

GOD'S Re-creative Power

Chaos described the state of my heart because I had no idea of what GOD was doing or why. All I knew was that everything was out of place. This upside-down living was most evident on Sundays. As a pastor, Sundays are the highlight of the week. A pastor spends a great deal of time and energy preparing for that day. During this disorienting time, there was no highlight. Sundays were almost like another day. It was a struggle to attend worship because we did not belong anywhere. Some weeks we did not even go. It is not that we did not want to go; we longed to attend and belong to a local church. Yet when we would attend, it was like a broken record, because every church seemed to be like every other one. Do not take that statement to be an accusation against any church. I was angry and disappointed at GOD. I was struggling to hear from Him. Which church would be authentic enough to embrace that kind of raw emotion? Was I ready to be embraced? I felt disheartened and nothing about church gave me hope. It felt like a place for "normal" people, those who had found their way in life and had it all together. And there I was, disoriented and confused.

I did not know that GOD was remodeling my life in a deep way. He was making me into someone new. This principle is seen throughout the New Testament. We read of it in 2 Corinthians 4:16:

Therefore we do not lose heart. Though outwardly we are wasting away, yet inwardly we are being renewed day by day.

We read of it in Ephesians 4:22-23:

You were taught . . . to be made new in the attitude of your minds

We read of the transforming process in Romans 12:2:

Do not conform to the pattern of this world, but be transformed by the renewing of your mind

We read of GOD'S creative process in the life of Abraham in Genesis. When GOD renewed His covenant relationship with Abraham after 23 years of silence, He gave him a new name,

"No longer will you be called Abram; your name will be Abraham."

Abram's new name meant "father of many." The promise of GOD from many years earlier was coming to pass. Things were changing for him. GOD was doing something new.

It was more than an empty promise. The name change was a reflection of what GOD had been doing inside of Abraham for many years. He had been making him. When GOD called him to leave his home, GOD was making him. When Abraham and his nephew Lot had to separate, GOD was making him. When Abraham had to rescue Lot, GOD was making Him. When Abraham and Sarah waited ten years for a child and nothing happened, GOD was making him. When they took things into their own hands and had a child by the handmaiden, GOD was making him. When GOD was silent for another thirteen years, GOD was making Him. And when GOD spoke to Abraham renewing the covenant, GOD was making him. Everything that had happened to Abraham up to this point was an expression of GOD'S creativity. GOD was creating something new inside of Abraham. He was making him a father of many.

Every Day A New Day

GOD creates. That is what He does and that is who He is. We see His creativity through the seasons of the years. Spring passes to summer that passes to autumn that passes to winter. Each season is an expression of new colors and climates. We see His creativity in the birth of children. Every single day, thousands of children breathe their first breaths due to the creative nature of GOD. And animals, including birds, amphibians, reptiles and mammals, are born every single day of the year, expressing the creative nature of GOD. New plants take root in forests and jungles all around the globe because of GOD'S creativity. He did not create a universe that was stagnant. Instead, it is a universe that has creativity written all over its DNA. GOD created a universe that grows and changes and creates. It expresses His creative nature.

Even when things appear to be destroyed, GOD's universe is capable of creating life where destruction has ruined everything. Perhaps you have heard of fireweed. When wildfires spread and destroy forests, this flower begins to grow and restore vegetation. During World War 2, the plant became widespread in Great Britain because it would grow in craters caused by bombs. When Mt. St. Helens in Washington erupted in May 1980, fireweed began appearing around the mountain within just a few months. Fireweed is a reminder of the creativity of GOD. When everything seems to be destroyed and forever gone, GOD is still creating. He is making something new out of nothing.

The only problem was that I could not see that. Unless you understand that things are being transformed for a better future, none of it makes sense. GOD was making something new out of me, but I did not know it. I felt like my life had erupted like a volcano, leaving a landscape that was barren and dead. I did not know that GOD was creating something.

An Inside Job

I did not realize a very important principle in the re-shaping creative process of GOD: a new future requires new thoughts. Just like our kitchen, my life needed to be turned upside-down. GOD wanted to create something new inside of me. The old way of thinking always takes us to the old way of living; therefore I needed a new way of thinking. And it was a deep, significant work, more than I ever imagined that I needed. Read the Message paraphrase of Ephesians 3:20:

"God can do anything, you know—far more than you could ever imagine or guess or request in your wildest dreams! He does it not by pushing us around but by working within us, his Spirit deeply and gently within us."

GOD wanted to do immeasurably more in me than I even knew to ask. I could not ask for it because I could not conceive what He had in mind. In order for me to grasp His purposes, He had to change me at the core of my being. He had to change my thought life. It was a significant remodeling project that would radically change the way I prayed, read Scripture, led others, talked, listened and followed Him. Just like Abraham, GOD was making me. In His silence, He was making me. In those unanswered prayers, He was making me. In my disappointments, He was making me. In my fears, He was making me. During this whole time of disorientation, GOD was making me. In order for Him to do immeasurably more around me meant that He had to do immeasurably more in me. And that kind of work does not happen overnight.

Discussion Questions

1. What are some losses you've experienced in life? How did they positively affect you?

2. How have your challenges in life created new ways of thinking?

3. What do you think about this statement:

"GOD wanted to do immeasurably more in me than I even knew to ask."

Have you ever experienced GOD creating a character trait in you that you did not even know you needed?

The Dance of the Falling Leaf

I am watching the leaves fall off a tree at Riverfront Park. There is a cool breeze rustling the canopy covering the path by the river. I watch one particular leaf as it falls to the earth. The descent seems to take forever. Rather than drop like a rock, it glides and flitters and sways, almost as a dance, as if to say, "Even in my dying, I will live."

The leaf is less than six months old. Such a short life. Why was it here? What purpose did it serve? Did such a brief appearance on earth really make a difference? Did its green color add any attractiveness to the park? Did it contribute to nature's beauty along the river? Did its connection to the tree give shade and comfort to lovers walking hand in hand along the path? Shouldn't that leaf continue to live?

And yet, watch the aging of the leaf. Does it not become even more beautiful in its orange and red hues? Even in its death, is there something beautiful? Is there something beneficial? Does not that one leaf, along with a million others, cover the ground giving nourishment to the soil from whence it came?

And then to discover that the dying process of the leaf is more than just dying. Yes, it was pushed. GOD designed nature to move forward and to create new life. The coming seasons call forth new life from the tree, and the growing process actually pushes off the old leaves from the previous season. In the colder climates, the leaves would catch the falling snow if they remained on the tree. As a result, limbs would break and damage the tree itself. However without the leaves, the tree is better able to live a fruitful life when spring arrives.

We see the grander scheme of things at work in the falling of this leaf. The forces of the universe are revealed even in the smaller things. The earth is rotating and revolving as it has done for millennia in such a way that in a few months, new leaves will appear on the tree again, grow and thrive for about six months and then, once again, they will dance to the ground in a final display of beauty.

Jesus at the Wheel

Have you ever ridden with someone to a place you did not know? If a friend were to say to you, "Get in and come with me," you would probably ask, "where?" If he were to say, "I will let you know. Just come with me," you would most likely get in the car and go because you trusted him. If the trip took ten minutes, your anxiety level would not go very high. If it lasted two hours, you would begin to question the trustworthiness of your friend. If you two stopped to spend the night because your journey was a two-day affair, the depth of your friendship would go to a new level. He knew where you were going, but he did not tell you. All you had was the relationship on which to base your trust.

That was the kind of trip GOD had planned for me. He was taking me to a new place, but did not bother to tell me about it. I did not have time to pack or tell anyone. I did not know where or why I was going. I had no idea how long it would last. I felt lost in my darkness traveling down a path that was rugged and harsh. Nothing was familiar. It was a road in the wilderness, one I had never traveled. In fact, no man had ever traveled this road because before that day, the road did not even exist.

The Moving Truck

Don't get me wrong. I wanted to go somewhere. I wanted GOD to move us to a new place. For several years, our computer monitor had a picture of a moving truck on it. Every morning that picture was one of the first things we saw. It was an encouraging reminder to us that a day was coming when a moving truck would pull in the driveway and take us and all of our possessions away to another place. During this time, we had several friends who moved. We helped some of them pack and when we drove away, we would think, "Well, next time that will be us." I was in a small group of guys who met weekly during this time. All of us wanted to move. In fact, we named our group "The LANDI Club." LANDI meant "Leave Albany Now Dang It!" All of them moved. I did not. My goal was to move. And GOD's goal for me was to move. However His idea of moving and my idea of moving were very different. His idea of moving was more spiritual and emotional. His idea was obviously better than mine.

In my years of following Jesus, I had traveled in certain ruts. I appreciated those ruts because they were smooth. I knew where to slow down and where I could speed up. I felt secure in those ruts. Few surprises caught me off-guard. I knew how to pray. I knew how to read the Bible. I knew how to fast. I knew how to lead Bible studies. I knew how to worship. Why would I need a new road? I was happy with my well-worn ruts. However, GOD was taking me to a new destiny and my ruts were taking me to old places, places where I was content and comfortable. They were places of my past, places that were familiar and secure. In order to get me to His chosen place, GOD had to open up a new road in the wilderness.

Building a New Road

Like a remodeling project, new road construction is a major ordeal. A new road requires the cutting down of trees, the clearing of underbrush and the smoothing of the land. All of that important stuff becomes debris because it is in the way of the road. It must be taken out. In the process, the entire forest is disrupted because every animal, insect and plant feels the impact of a new road. The root system of the trees is radically affected. The animals must create new trails. The presence of new animals, a.k.a. humans, in the forest is unnerving. The birds must look for new nesting places. Even the insects lose their normal routine. In a word, it is chaos.

This task does not happen overnight. It is long and tedious and upsetting. It was for me. At one time, my wilderness was settled. I had followed Jesus for more than 40 years, but now all of a sudden He wanted to turn it all upside down. He found a very unwilling and impatient protester in the forest. I had tied myself to a tree. "Save the trees!" I chanted. I was fighting GOD'S new work. But why? Why was I fighting His work? He loves me more than I love me. Why couldn't I trust Him?

Most people do not embrace change. They like the stability of the status quo. However, I am not a person of habits. Instead, I like adventure. But this trek was not a trip I wanted to take. What was causing me to object to this new journey? The main challenge confronting me was fear, mainly of the unknown. First, I was unsure how involved GOD was in this process. Was it really Him at work here or was it my own doing? Second, I did not know where this new road was going. What would the destination look like and did I really want to go there? Third, I did not know how long this would take. In a race, the finish line is critical because you know how much farther you have. In this race, I had no idea when I would finish. Fourth, I feared what I would lose. The assurance of my life's purpose was that GOD had created and gifted me to pastor. I wondered if perhaps I had disqualified myself from GOD'S calling. If so, what would I do? Fifth, I feared that we would not make it financially, emotionally, or relationally. Fear was a part of this darkness and it was all over me.

Looking for Stuckey's

I felt that the longer the trip lasted, the less certain I was that I would finish. The only certainty I had was that GOD was still GOD. Whatever He chose to do was beyond my control. The only thing I could do was trust Him. I came to the same conclusion as Jesus' disciples did in John 6:68, *"Lord to whom shall we go? You have the words of eternal life."* That thought permeated my prayers and thoughts regularly. I had nowhere else to go. If Jesus was still willing to take me with all my baggage, then I was willing to go with Him.

Jesus cut a new road in the wilderness with bumps and holes and curves and cliffs. It had steep grades and sharp turns. He did not really bother to smooth it out much. He knew that He could not drive me very fast down this new road. He knew that I would whine and ask for Him to pull over, that I was feeling sick, that I needed to go to the bathroom, that I was hungry, that we were lost, and on and on and on. Jesus knew that I would ask to go back to the way things were. He knew I was unsure that I could trust Him on this trip. And Jesus was right. He knew it would last longer and go further than I expected or wanted. So why bother making it straight and flat? He knew that I would never go there had He not come to my wilderness and said, "Let's go." But that day in my lostness, it is like He drove up to my house, opened the car door and just looked at me. I stood objecting. He did not really say anything. What does one do with that kind of invitation? You get in, sit down, buckle up and hold on.

When I was growing up, we would travel occasionally to see our extended family who lived about two hours away. It involved a short trip on the interstate. One of the places we kids enjoyed stopping was Stuckey's. It was one of those tourist stores that had snacks and souvenirs. I still remember the pecan logs they sold. They looked delicious. However, I do not remember ever getting one – not even for Christmas! Anyway, we would occasionally stop so we could get out of the car. To a boy with a small bladder, that sign was a welcomed relief. And riding in a car for a whole hour is boring to a kid. We would look for the Stuckey's sign to know how much farther we had to go.

Unfortunately with Jesus at the wheel, road signs are scarce. In my case, the lack of signs meant that I had no idea where I was going or how much further to our destination. And that was a good thing. If I had known where it was taking me, I would have run if He had stopped at the Stuckey's. In fact, I tried to run. Jesus was taking me to deep places of my heart. I did not want to go to those places. And yet I am grateful that He took me there and I am even more grateful that He stayed with me as long as I needed to be there. Like the good shepherd of Psalm 23, He did not leave me to face my trials alone. Jesus, our Shepherd, went with me.

"Even though I walk through the valley of the shadow of death, I will fear no evil, for You are with me."

That valley where death overshadows us is deep. It is fearful. Fortunately, it is not permanent. It is a place through which we pass, not a place where we stay. Jesus carried me to those places to uncover and recover my heart. The wounds of my past were revealed and the powerful healing of Jesus began the restoring process. He took me to a new depth of wholeness.

Get In, Buckle Up and Hold On

What were those deep places? They were issues of my heart related to my past, my family, my idols, my fears and my failures. As He and I traveled down the road through the wilderness, it was like Jesus would stop and get out. He would wave at me to come to where He was and I would get out and stand next to Him. Then He would push back the underbrush to reveal stuff I had kept hidden from others and even from myself. He would not shake His head in disappointment or speak to me in rebuke. Instead Jesus would look at me with His eyes full of powerful grace and simply say, "I want more for you than that." And then without saying a word, the invitation to let go of that stuff was obvious. Of course I wanted to let it go, but I was not sure I could. He knew that because He would then say, "Look at Me. Do you not see that I am enough to set you free from this? It is up to you." And then I was faced with a choice of the old ruts of my security or the treacherous road to a new destiny.

Once again I saw that GOD was not interested in behavior modification. He wanted to do more than change the way I behaved. He wanted to change the way I thought and perceived and understood and desired. He wanted to change my heart because the heart is the source of everything we do, think and feel. The wisdom of Proverbs 4:23 is evident:

"Above all else, guard your heart, for everything you do flows from it."

The reason we do what we do is because of what is in our hearts. We steal because our hearts want to have as much as we think others have. We misbehave sexually because of our heart's desires to be held and cherished. We lie because our hearts tell us that others will think less of us if we are truthful. We don't treat others kindly because our hearts do not want to appear weak. Our actions come from our hearts. Therefore GOD wants to take us to those places where the brokenness of our hearts is revealed.

However, we are challenged because very few of us want to go w/ Him to those places. It is easier to live in the secure ruts of a broken road rather than risk traveling a new road to fearful places, even with Jesus there. Our hearts deceive us and tell us that we risk rejection from Him or from others. That is what I thought.

Through the Desert

This journey of discovery is rarely enjoyable. It involves revelations of hidden thoughts, perceptions, feelings and fears. And yet it is necessary. In order to experience the more that Jesus offers us, we need to let go of the "less" that is hidden in our hearts. Os Hillman wrote:

As we have seen, Scripture uses Egypt as a symbol for slave and toil. Egypt is our past. The Promised Land is our future. But there is a wilderness between the two. The road to the Promised Land always leads through the desert.[viii]

We cannot stay in Egypt and hope for the Promised Land. If we are to move into tomorrow, we must leave our yesterday. That transition takes us through a wilderness of faith wanderings. It is a road that feels disorienting. It was for me. I felt lost and uncertain. I saw His footprints only briefly and yet those moments were powerful encouragers that kept me on the road He was laying out before me.

What were those deep places that Jesus took me to? What did He reveal to me?

Discussion Questions

1. Difficult times can be revealing moments in life. Can you recall a difficult time where you saw your own heart more clearly? What did you see?

2. What are the new things GOD:

- Has done in you during the past five years? One year?

- Is doing in you right now?

3. Do you struggle with allowing Jesus to drive your life? If so, what fears keep Him out of the seat?

A Heart Disconnected

Before I take you to my heart, let me tell you how I got it. For all of my life, I had kept most of my heart to myself. No one had bothered to ask me about the secrets of my safe place. I had years of thoughts, dreams and fears I had never told anyone because no one had ever asked me. I certainly was not going to initiate that conversation either. After all, what man wants to be found out that perhaps he is not enough? And yes, I did assume that I was not enough because no one ever told me that I was enough.

In the Shadow of the Depression

My parents were great people. They were products of the depression era. Growing up where food and necessities were in limited supply gave them a "provider" understanding of parenting. They worked hard to make sure their children had food to eat, clothes to wear and a place to sleep. And they were great providers. We were not wealthy by many standards, but we had enough. I am grateful every day that my parents were willing to sacrifice for the sake of their four children. I am grateful for a mother who was willing to keep working in order to pay my college tuition. For them, taking care of physical needs took precedence over emotional needs. I can only remember one conversation where someone asked me what was on my heart. As a result, I never learned to connect with my own heart. I never saw it and I was never taught it.

I think it was the common path of most men who were raised in the seventies. Our fathers taught us to work hard and to make financial provision for our families. And that is a great lesson. However, many of us did not learn about emotional provision. Which of us had someone to tap us on the chest regularly and ask, "Hey bud, what's going on in there?" Which of us had a trusted individual to enter into our world? As a result, we grew up ignoring the stuff inside. The term "detached heart" comes to mind. We were unknowingly taught to develop an internal safe house where we could store the secret things of our hearts, things such as our feelings, ideas, fears and dreams.

Best-selling authors Henry Cloud and John Townsend have devoted their counseling ministry to helping others. In their book, *How People Grow*, Townsend points out that our relational challenges often stem from the failure to connect with one's own heart.

"A man may realize his parents have been unresponsive emotionally to him all his life. He may see how this unresponsiveness has made his relational life difficult, as he has not been connected enough to his inner self to connect with others."[ix]

We were taught, mostly unintentionally, that men are strong and independent. We did not need to tell anybody anything because we had it covered. Asking for help meant weakness. We were taught to wear the mask of independence. Look strong. Be enough.

Am I Enough?

However, every young man's heart asks the question: What if I am not enough? What if I don't succeed? What if I am afraid? To compensate for our perceived inadequacies, we created a false self that we could portray to the world. We created an outward expression of ourselves that we relied on for safety and success, and we hid the true self from those around us and even from ourselves. For some, it meant working harder than others or getting a law degree or earning an athletic scholarship. As long as we excelled ahead of others, we did not need to explain anything. We were safe

For others, we created a false self of addictions or homelessness or obesity. We were taught to blame others or to depend on others so that we would never be held responsible. We learned to manipulate our situations so that we were not required or expected to do anything to change it. We had nothing to offer so we could live irresponsibly. It was not our fault.

I developed a false-self and became comfortable with it. It defined me. People knew me by that pretension. And it made up the wilderness where Jesus came to me. I had created a wonderful oasis where everything was safe and satisfying. It was my false-self. And I was content. And then one day the leaves on the bushes began to wither. Something was happening to my hideout. I awakened from my comfort nap to find Jesus standing there. With a smile on His face and hands on His hips, He asked, "Really? Are you satisfied living as a pretender?" I dropped my lemonade and the background music screeched to a halt. "Follow Me," He said and with the swing of His machete, the low branches of a tree fell to the ground. He began the construction of a road that would lead me out of my hideout into a new future.

A Safe Audience

What did that invitation look like? Soon after leaving the church plant, my wife, Kim, and I went on a week-long retreat for wounded pastors. For the first time, I was encouraged and enabled to look inside my true self. With the help of my wife and a gifted counselor, I was able to begin talking about things related to my past, my family and my own heart. It was a freeing experience, but it was incredibly challenging.

I have never been more grateful for a wife I could trust than I was during this disorienting season. Over the years, we have maintained our uniqueness on the one hand, and yet our hearts have become so intertwined that we are one. I knew that I could trust Kim's heart. During this season, she asked me the questions that allowed me to start uncovering my camouflaged heart. I was beginning to see myself in a whole new light. She gave me a safe audience where I could take the risk of seeing who I was and then telling someone else. And she prodded me without nagging me. In the words of John Eldredge, I married a woman who did more than "make me feel like a man; she challenged me to be one."[x]

Going through this season together was a defining moment for our marriage. Both of us were in this season of uncertainty and we chose each day to go through this road construction process together. Jesus was cutting a new road for her future, too. We both had some of the same questions, and we were able to ask those questions because we were in the same place. We understood the nagging doubts that waited for us to awaken each morning and then sat on our shoulders all day long. We knew what it was like to struggle to carry the weight of feeling forgotten and worthless. Fortunately, we chose not to take out our anger on each other. We told GOD about our anger.

Indeed this season was not a pleasant time for either one of us. However, the benefits of it cannot be adequately described. We had more significant and difficult conversations than ever before. We had to deal with serious issues. And in this process GOD was not only strengthening our marriage, He was reorienting and deepening our marriage. Both of us were being made new. GOD was preparing to take us to places we could not imagine. Those places would require more than we had and more than we were. It was becoming a beautiful thing.

Don't Go Back

The challenge for me was not to return to my hidden oasis. It was so secure. Its attraction was magnetic. While Jesus was taking me to a new place, the comfort of who I had been was also calling me to return. Its voice was loud. I loved Jesus, but I also enjoyed the secret heart of my past. I had to keep pressing on towards the future. It was easy for me to look back to my former place of comfort and security. Jesus was calling me to follow Him. He wanted me to trust Him to be my security and my comfort. I was learning to depend on Him rather than my false self.

And once I discovered and recovered my heart, I was able to identify who I was. And from that discovery I began to live authentically out of a deep, connected heart.

Discussion Questions

1. Has anyone ever communicated to you that you are enough? Or not enough? How?

2. Cloud and Townsend wrote:

> *"A man may realize his parents have been unresponsive emotionally to him all his life.*
> *He may see how this unresponsiveness has made his relational life difficult, as he has not been connected enough to his inner self to connect with others."*

Have you experienced an inability to connect with others due to the lack of connection with your own heart? If so, how?

3. Have you ever recognized a false self in someone else? What was the tip off?

Do you have a false self? How do you see it?

4. Who are the individuals who could help you uncover your false self?

A Heart Discovered

What was my heart? My detached heart had been covered up and was laden with layers of hidden dreams and fears. My authentic heart was one where my secrets were laid bare, where I owned up to who I truly was. It meant that I could be my true self. It meant living life from the core of who I truly was, not from the essence of who I thought others would want me to be.

Once I grasped this realization (that I could be who GOD made me to be), I was able to turn a corner. Instead of trying to be someone that made a positive impression on others, I learned to live with who I was. And I realized that who I was was enough. In fact, living authentically was a powerful life. The refusal to attempt false impressions was the start to a life that made a more profound impact on the world around me. I did not have to try to be like someone else. GOD did not make me to be them. Instead He made me to be me. And when I lived like me, then He could express His life through me. I was becoming an authentic vessel through which Jesus could reveal Himself to the people around me.

How did I turn that corner? How did I overcome my concerns of what others may think of me? The main thing was my awareness of this powerful voice within. Once I became conscious about my posing, I confronted my own heart. I no longer had to impress others. Awareness of my people pleasing mentality was what broke the chains of bondage. As I lived with that awareness, I simply refused to do what I thought others wanted me to do. I chose to live an authentic life of following Jesus. A memorable quote from John Eldredge that encouraged me was:

"Let people feel the weight of who I am . . ." [xi]

I learned how to speak the truth in love (Ephesians 4:15). And I could let others deal with how that would affect them. I refused to own their response. Instead I chose to live out of an authentic heart that was learning to refuse fear's controlling presence.

During this disorienting season of life, I can put into words a few of the transformations that took place in my heart. These changes did not happen overnight. Over a process of time, I saw them take root. What did they look like?

My Connected Heart – Humble Confidence

As my lostness plunged me into the depths of my heart, I saw more clearly who I was and as a result, I was able to begin serving and leading from the confidence of my true-self rather than from the fear of my false-self. I did not realize that for many years I had been partially leading from a sense of insecurity rather than courage. I saw this insecurity from the several occasions I would ride by another church in the community and think, "Those guys are doing well. I wonder why I can't do that?" I was not jealous of them, but I just felt this inadequacy inside to lead my church to becoming a greater church.

Since coming through the disorienting season where I was able to connect to my own heart, I have learned to accept my giftedness from GOD rather than wish for different gifts. I am thankful for who I am and grateful that GOD continues to make me more than I am. I refuse to compare myself to other leaders. I am learning that by the grace of GOD, I am enough and that I do not have to compare myself to others to measure my effectiveness as a leader. And I am learning to lead in humble dependence on GOD. I am learning how to lean heavily on His power to work powerfully through my life to accomplish immeasurably more than I can imagine.

It is humble confidence that has overtaken my heart and swallowed my pride and insecurity. I am confident in who GOD is and what GOD is doing in me and through me rather than in what I am doing. I do not measure myself based on numbers or how pleased people are with my ministry. I do not confuse my worth with my performance. Regardless of the outcomes, I am no less significant. I have confidence regardless of the perceived progress based on human measurements. The words of 2 Corinthians 3:5 have been great encouragement to me:

> *Not that we are competent in ourselves*
> *to claim anything for ourselves,*
> *but our competence comes from GOD.*

Learning to live and lead from the competence that comes from GOD has been a game changer. It has given me great joy to follow, watch and celebrate what GOD is doing through me.

My Connected Heart – A Wife to Trust

My wife and I have always had a solid, healthy relationship. We have communicated well, spent time together and helped each other for many years. During the reorienting season of life, all of that went to a deeper level. One of our sayings that came from our lostness was a simple idea, "We are in this together." That is the way this whole deal started. We planted the church as a family and we left the church as a family. We entered this season of life as a family. We endured as a family. Sink or swim, we would do so together.

And when our plans were pulled out from under us, the incredible value of family rose up. Did the stress cause Kim and me to have difficult conversations? Yes. Did the challenges cause us to be angry and frustrated? Yes. Did we always like each other? No. Did we wonder if life would be easier apart from each other? Yes. But we always came back to the same answer – We need each other. In the midst of this dark night of the soul, we learned to reach out in the darkness for the other's hand. Feeling those fingers grasp my own made things better. I had someone standing with me. She was someone who knew me better than anyone. She knew my weakness and faults and failures. And every time I reached out my hand for hers, it was there. And I mean every time. Never once did I look for her that she had turned around and walked away.

This dark night brought strength to our relationship. One reason the darkness was such a powerful time of restoration was because I was no longer operating from a façade. My uncovered and authentic heart was reconnected to her. As I learned more of who I was, I was able to offer more of who I was to her, rather than the cheap and shallow surface.

Perhaps this part is what I treasure the most about this disorienting time. Our relationship as husband and wife will be the one experience that will last me until my last breath on earth. Several years ago, I heard someone say that a pastor needs to keep their families first because he will wake up one day and the church will no longer be a part of his life. However, the pastor will never wake up a single day when his spouse is not a part of his life. By the grace of GOD, I will be a faithful husband until death do us part.

My Connected Heart - Transparency

My personality has what I call "complementary weaknesses." Let me explain. Throughout my life I have wanted to please others. I am one of those non-confrontational individuals. I have not been one to start arguments and have avoided them where I could. The other challenge I faced was that I did not think quickly on my feet. I have been more of a plodder, planning ahead & dealing with issues thoughtfully. Over the years, I have discovered that these two go hand in hand. I have seen how they fed each other. Therefore I have often swallowed my feelings or my response to situations because either I did not know what to say or I did not want to confront someone. And then after thinking about the issue, I would occasionally decide the best course of action and then do nothing about it.

As I walked through this disorienting season I began to deal with these challenges. I realized that I could not continue swallowing my feelings and refusing to confront things because of my people pleaser mindset. GOD was developing in me the courage and determination to let these things no longer sway me from being more than I could be.

I remember a friend inviting me to attend church with him. Honestly, it was a church that we did not care to attend. During our conversation, I gave him a nice, non-committal response, "Well maybe we can." But my friend continued to press for an answer. Finally I said, "You know what, I need to be honest with you. I appreciate your asking. But we are not coming. I don't want you to expect us to come when I know that we will not come." I am not sure if he appreciated my honesty, but I was glad that I could be transparent. Trying to please my friend faded into the background for me while being authentic became the center. Honesty and niceness can often co-exist. But there are times when we need to be honest with people and tell them the truth. Those conversations are not always nice, but they can be helpful and full of love. Sometimes the most un-loving thing we can do is to be nice.

In this discovery process, I experienced the power of transparency to connect with people. Our hearts yearn for authenticity. Our realness connects with others. The transparent soul does not run others away. Instead, it draws them like a magnet. Authentic people can be trusted.

My Connected Heart – Compassionate Communication

Being lost is a life changing experience affecting every area of one's life. One area it touched deeply was my preaching. That process began when I jumped into the church planting world. Starting a church to reach people who do not go to church brought many questions to the surface, questions I had never asked before. Questions like:

Do I need to give money if I come to church?

Will you call on me to pray out loud?

And the more thoughtful questions they asked:

Do you want me to attend for my sake or for your sake? When I stepped away from the church plant and began attending worship as a broken and lost individual, everything sounded different. A broken heart hears and sees things differently. I did. When I had the opportunity to preach again, I saw things in a whole new light. I preached with more passion and compassion. My heart longed to communicate the restoring grace of GOD to people. I no longer looked at a gathered congregation as people needing to be corrected. Instead

I saw brokenness and fear. I saw people struggling to make it through another day. I saw people who felt they had failed GOD. That understanding was only deepened as I walked with hospice families. I saw them grieve the deaths of their family members. I walked with them through the valley of the shadow of death. I felt with them. While I did not understand the loss of a child or a spouse, I did understand loss. In some ways, I was grieving too. And when I preached I knew that the congregation had many listeners who were lost or grieving or weary. My speaking was marked by encouragement, hope and compassion. The words of Philo, first-century philosopher, became central to my ministry:

> *"Be kind for everyone you meet is fighting a great battle."*[xii]

My focus became how I could help them fight and win those battles. I knew what it was like. I was fighting a battle too.

When GOD Shows Up Through Me

Through all of this I came to grasp this one huge reality that changed my future –

The most powerful life I can live is the life of authenticity.

I came to peace with the fact that I could not be anyone else. Though I had often compared myself to others through the years and wondered why I could not do what they could do, I realized how skewed that thinking was. If GOD had intended for me to be someone else, He would have made me someone else. But GOD intended for me to be me, and the best way I could honor Him and make an impact on the world around me was to live the life He had created me to live. Trying to be someone else or to do something else was a complete failure. I needed to become all that GOD had made me by reaching the full potential of His creative desires. He had a plan for my life and that plan was for me to be a powerful expression of His presence in this world. And if I did not live out that calling, then I was missing the point of my being here. GOD knew that the world needed the truest expression of me so He made me.

Jessi Marquez was a young college student on a journey similar to my own. She was looking for her heart. GOD was looking for her. Her journey was literal while mine was internal. She left the United States to serve others and found herself talking with prostitutes in Malaysia, caring for children in the Philippines, and serving women in Kenya. And in her journey across the oceans, she discovered her own heart. It was a heart that cared for those imprisoned by injustice and forgotten by the rest of the world. Jessi discovered the desires of her heart and in the process, the true Jessi Marquez came to the surface. She realized that her authentic heart was a clear and powerful expression of GOD that liberates the world. She wrote, "It is when people don't allow GOD to show up through them that the world collapses in on itself."[xiii]

As I read of Jessi's journey, I knew that I wanted GOD to show up through me. That has been the desire of my heart for decades. I just needed to uncover my heart and embrace it fully.

My heart began to long to become all that GOD had made me to become. I was not there yet, but by GOD'S grace I was on the road of becoming. I was willing for GOD to peel away the layers of hiddenness, uncover my heart and then destroy the obstacles that stood in the

way of His calling on my life. My prayer became,
"GOD, whatever is hindering me from reaching the full
potential for which you made me, change. If it is my
habits or pride or self-centeredness, or thought patterns
or fears or relationships that are standing in the way of
my living the best life possible, then change all of that. I
want to live the fullness of Your plans for my life and I
am willing to give up everything that stands in the way
of Your purposes for my life."

And it dawned on me that it is rarely the external
forces that hinder us from being all that GOD made us to
be. The obstacles that we usually face are on the inside.
Even though efforts to thwart GOD'S plan for my life
were from without, it was my response to them that
determined whether I would overcome them. That is
when this disorienting season of life finally began to
make sense. GOD really had been making me like He
had done Abraham.

Discussion Questions

1. How have your difficult seasons of life changed you?
How are you more –

Courageous?	Resilient?
Hopeful?	Forgiving?
Passionate?	Gracious?

How are you more –

Uncertain?	Afraid?
Self-protective?	Impatient?
Pessimistic?	Bitter?

2. *"The most powerful life I can live is the life of authenticity."*

How have you seen the power of your life through your transparency?

3. Why do you think an authentic life is so compelling?

4. Why do we embrace someone else's authenticity while we hide our own?

"One More"
Bruce Pittman

One more day,
One more step,
I will press on,
I will run this race.
I keep going.
I will finish this course.

I will keep the faith.

No cross will stop me.
Hope is the fuel of my flame.
Sometimes the flame becomes a flicker
 My Father has called me to this moment.
And I do not want to take another step
I will lay aside
Or go another day.
Every weight,
But still I do.
Every obstacle.

Almost there
His strength will suffice,
Stay focused.
I will finish well.

One step at a time.
One more day,
One more step,
The long stretch ahead is difficult,
I keep going.
It is hard. It is hot.

The future is an uphill climb.
The heat drains my energy,
But I can't stop now.
I must keep moving.
I will finish.

I lift my foot.
I step forward.
Quitting is not a choice.
Stop thinking about it.
Take another step.
That step takes me closer to the finish.
I am closer now than I've ever been.

But where will my strength come from?
How can I press on?
The pain is greater.
The heaviness is too much.
Why must the end be a climb?

Running the Race

"This is ridiculous," I thought to myself. "Why in the world can't I finish this? I have run this far before. What is going on?" During my season of lostness, I had begun enjoying long-distance running (Yes, I used the word "enjoying" to define running). Running gave me a great time to pray and think. It was also a challenge to see how far I could run. I was hoping to do more than a marathon. On this run, I was attempting to surpass twenty miles. It was my third attempt. I had accomplished it before. But now that I began pressing toward twenty-three miles, I found myself giving out at eighteen miles and walking the rest of the way home. In fact, my wife became worried about me one morning and came looking for me. I rode home with her. I was frustrated and disappointed.

Running Lessons

Running taught me valuable lessons. One lesson was that running is more psychological than it is physical. Yes a person needs to have strong legs and lungs. He needs to strengthen the ankles, knees and hips. However, if the mind does not have the capacity to keep running, the rest of it does not matter. Endurance is a matter of the heart.

I also learned that there is a world of difference between a half-marathon and a marathon and the difference is more than just distance. Running a half-marathon was a fairly easy accomplishment for me. I accomplished that feat in a few months of training. However the full marathon was more than just running. I had to think more about my eating habits, my sleeping routine and other things that were not an issue with the half-marathon. I had to contend with "the wall" that did not appear when running a half-marathon. I found out that a twenty-six mile run would require of me more than I had. And that was exactly what GOD was teaching me and training me to do. It was much more than I imagined.

Life is a Race; Endure!

As I read the Bible, I found endurance everywhere. It seemed that every person who trusted GOD was called to endure. In Genesis, Joseph had to endure the trials of rejection, slavery, false accusations and imprisonment. It was at least thirteen years of endurance. Moses had to endure forty years of leading a rebellious group of people through the wilderness. Then he died and never even saw the finish line. Isaiah and many of the Old Testament prophets had to endure rejection and persecution when they spoke the word of the Lord. The early church endured hard times as they followed Jesus. Paul endured hardships as he composed most of his letters (and most of the New Testament) from filthy prisons. He used words such as "hard pressed, perplexed, persecuted, struck down and wasting away" (2 Corinthians 4:8-9) to describe his life as a disciple of Jesus. John endured many years of following Jesus, ending up exiled on an island in the Mediterranean (it was not a resort island).

Above all, however, we look to Jesus as the perfect model of endurance. We read that He *"endured the cross, scorning its shame"* and He *"endured such opposition from sinful men"* (Hebrews 12:2-3). Jesus set the example of endurance when He carried His cross through the streets of Jerusalem to Golgotha. Those few hours must have seemed like an eternity to Him. He endured words of false accusations. He endured innumerable fists to His jaw and face. The barbs in the whip ripped His flesh repeatedly. The crown of thorns that was pressed deeply into his head caused searing pain. Every nerve in His body must have cried out for relief. Along with all of that painful torture, Jesus had to carry the cross. I don't know how he was physically able to take another step. I am astonished when I think that He was even able to pick up a cross, much less carry it uphill. How much more could this man go? And Roman soldiers still had not even crucified Him! Then came the nails in the hands and feet. The pain of such a moment is beyond comprehension, yet Jesus took all of that. He walked every single step. He endured every moment of that experience.

Jesus, Enduring Man

The one thought that seals the enduring strength of Jesus comes from His own mouth. It was the moment when Judas brought the soldiers to the Garden of Gethsemane to arrest Jesus secretly. Surrounded by the Temple guards, Peter pulled out his sword and began the fight to defend Jesus. With one swipe, he separated an ear from its head (Personally, I think he was attempting to sever the head from the shoulders). But Jesus stopped the fight before it even got started.

"Put your sword back in its place . . . Do you think I cannot call on my Father, and He will at once put at my disposal more than twelve legions of angels?"
Matthew 26:53

At any time, I believe that Jesus could have simply thought, "Father, get Me out of this." But He did not. Jesus had the means of escape from this disastrous moment. However, he refused to take that route. Instead Jesus set His mind to finish and He walked every single, terrible, painful step that took Him to an even worse ending – His crucifixion. Then Jesus watched as they tied his hands and feet to the cross. He felt them apply pressure to his inner forearms and then the sharp point of the nail in his wrist. The pain caused by the driving of the nails must have been unspeakable. The angels in heaven watched in eager anticipation that Jesus would speak the word, "Rescue Me." But He refused. Instead, He endured every moment of that experience. He hung there for six long, dreadful hours. Jesus would not quit. Instead He finished. He was faithful to the end. When I consider what Jesus did, I am in awe of what it took for Him to walk that path GOD had laid before Him. He showed us what it meant to endure.

Greater Mountains and Stronger Faith

And here I was in the middle of a time in life where I felt lost and uncertain. I had no idea where to go or what to do. I was learning to endure. All of the struggles I faced, the hills I climbed, and the obstacles I overcame were GOD'S methods of teaching and training me to press on to the end.

I had just never faced such difficulties before. I had never been challenged so deeply before. And the struggles I faced were not my circumstances. These struggles were issues from within my own heart. GOD was accomplishing two goals during this time of disorientation. He was revealing weakness and growing strength in my character. He was developing within me the capacity to endure. The primary way to develop endurance is to do just that – endure. That is how I was able to run long distances – by running long distances.

And slowly it began to dawn on me why GOD had not answered our prayers. I finally realized why He had been so quiet. He had greater plans in mind than just finding me a job. He was developing endurance in me, the thing that He desired for every leader from the Bible. As mentioned earlier, it is the one character trait we see repeated over and again throughout the reading of the Scripture. GOD was doing in me what He had done in others. I was learning how to *"run with perseverance the race marked out for us."* (Hebrews 12:1)

Overall this season in my life illustrates a principle we see in the Bible. It is this:

When GOD delays the answer to a prayer, it is because He is doing something greater than we even know to ask.

More Than You Know

Perhaps you have read the story of a young mother in the Old Testament who could not have children (1 Samuel 2). Her name was Hannah and she desperately longed for a child. She cried out to GOD repeatedly for the privilege of being a mother. The words used to describe her praying include "bitterness of soul, wept much, great anguish and grief." But they were to no avail. Samuel later wrote of his parents' visits to the Temple. He described her prayers to the Lord that went on year after year. GOD was delaying his answer to her request. How her heart must have yearned for the privilege of motherhood. Yet He had something greater in mind than just giving Hannah a child. Although a child would have been an enormous blessing to her,

GOD was thinking about something greater than that. He was thinking about His people, the nation of Israel. He saw that the upcoming leaders were *"wicked men; they had no regard for the Lord."* He saw that they would need a godly leader, a man who would love Him first and foremost. He saw kings in their future and they would need someone to choose those kings. If Hannah would be willing to dedicate that child to Him, then the greater picture of GOD'S plan would be completed. So He refused to answer the deepest desires of her heart until she had the capacity to surrender that child ahead of time to the Lord. It was an incredibly long journey for her, but when the race was over and the child was born, greater things were accomplished. They were things she never could have imagined.

The delay of GOD's response to our prayers may be indicating that He has something in mind that is greater than we can ask. Hannah could not have asked for what GOD wanted to do through Samuel. Neither can we ask for what GOD wants to do. We cannot even imagine it. Yet He brings us along to the place where we can surrender our own dreams for His greater dreams. And in the process He does something in us that is life changing.

For Abraham, enduring meant waiting out the silence. Abraham was seventy-five years old when he first heard the voice of the invisible GOD inviting him to go to a land that He would show him (Genesis 12:1). He did just that taking his wife, his nephew (Lot), their possessions and servants. The promise to Abraham was land and a family. At this point, they had no children (Barren wombs were a continual threat to GOD'S plans in the Old Testament). All they had was a promise and that was their situation for ten years – a promise with no results for ten long years. Have you ever waited for something for ten years?

Abraham and his wife decided to try for a family with their own ingenuity (See Genesis 16). Sarah came up with the idea of Abraham sleeping with her servant, Hagar. And it worked. Hagar became pregnant and then things went south quickly. Because of her pregnancy, Hagar began to look scornfully at Sarah and Sarah began to despise Hagar. Abraham was caught right in the middle of it all. In fact, Sarah actually blamed him for the whole debacle. *"You are responsible for the wrong I am suffering,"* she told him. I can imagine Abraham was ready to throw both of them out. Their best plans to accomplish GOD'S goal failed. And then it was another fourteen years before GOD did give Abraham and Sarah a son, Isaac. They waited twenty-four years for GOD to fulfill His promise to them.

The one lesson that drew my attention was the lesson on waiting. While Abraham waited on GOD to fulfill His word, his heart was revealed. GOD was shaping Abraham with silence and darkness. He was uncovering his unwillingness to wait on GOD regardless of how long it took and in the process his impatience surfaced.

The Revealing Silence of GOD

We learn that when GOD is silent, it could be that he is revealing our heart. That is what happened to me in the waiting. I began to see my heart more clearly. I saw the areas that were nothing more than cracks in my foundation. GOD knew that. The revelation was for my sake, not His. He already knew my heart, but the dark places were hidden from my own sight and that is what I needed to see when GOD was silent.

Our character is foundation to all that GOD desires to do through our lives. If the foundation has cracks in it, it will not withstand the tremendous pressure that comes from a great work. The waiting allows for the flaws and weaknesses to be revealed. We see more clearly why we are where we are. We also see how GOD wants to deepen us. Waiting allows the light to shine on the dark places. Richard Hendrix wrote,

"Second only to suffering, waiting may be the greatest teacher & trainer in godliness, maturity, & genuine spirituality most of us ever encounter."[xiv]

For me a big part of this challenging time was the fact that I did not know where the finish line was. A race always has a finish line. When I run, I usually have a good idea of how much further I have to run. But in this disorientation season, I had no idea where the end was. All I knew was to get up every day and keep moving forward. Neither Hannah nor Abraham had any idea when or if their race would be over. But GOD had a plan. He was fulfilling His dreams. And He would see to it that the desires of their hearts would be satisfied as well.

Once I learned that this was about endurance, I realized that I was no longer lost. I knew where I was, what was going on and where I was going.

Discussion Questions

1. Recall a time when you quit something because it was too hard.

What was that like? What was so hard about it that you quit? What lessons did you learn from quitting?

2. Can you recall a time when you prayed for GOD to get you out of something and He refused?

What was your response? Looking back now, how beneficial was His refusal?

3. What are the things that help you endure when life is hard?

4. Richard Hendrix wrote:

"Second only to suffering, waiting may be the greatest teacher & trainer in godliness, maturity, & genuine spirituality most of us ever encounter."

How have you experienced waiting as a lesson?

Back up from the Trees; See the Forest

It is easy to lose the forest for the trees. When I was going through my disorientation, I was so focused on the moments before me that I lost sight of how it all connected. All I could see was the tree before me. The darkness of my situation shrouded my sight from seeing what was behind me and what was ahead of me.

However, as I moved through the dark time and began to come out on the other side, I was able to look back and see how this season of life was a step in the journey on which GOD had been leading me ever since I was born. He was taking me to another stage in my life. I began to understand a simple truth: it's all connected. My past, my present and my future were all connected. Once I was able to see the bigger story that GOD was writing and the greater context of it all, I was able to accept where I was, what I was enduring, and where it all was headed. It really was going somewhere. My life was not a convening of random circumstances. GOD was growing me. GOD was taking me somewhere. His destiny for my life was in process. I could not go where He desired until I became what He desired. Once I saw the forest, I could live in the darkness.

A Larger Story

If we are to grasp the meaning of the situations that are confusing and dark, we need to understand that our situations, indeed our lives, are a part of a larger story. It is a story that GOD is writing. It is part of His plan that is unfolding (Jeremiah 29:11). Nowhere in the Bible do we read of any situation that was not connected to its past and its future. The Bible tells us of a flow of history that started with Adam and Eve, and culminated with the church. And all of it is connected. Adam was connected to Abraham who was connected to Moses who was connected to Isaiah who was connected to John the Baptist who was connected to Peter who was connected to Paul. In fact, every individual in the Bible, the known and unknown, is connected to every other individual and all of them are connected to you and me. All of it, including our own lives, is a part of the flow of GOD'S plan.

It is easy to see the connections in the Bible. However, when we are in the middle of a dark time, it is difficult to connect it with our past or our future. For instance, when we read those hair-raising adventures of Moses or the risky life of Jesus, why don't our hearts beat faster when things get dicey for them? Why don't we get anxious for Moses when he and his people are facing the Red Sea before them and Pharaoh's army behind them? Why aren't we nervous for Jesus when He is about to be arrested? It is because we know the end of the story. We know that the present event is connected to the past and the future. We know how it all comes together. What we don't think about is how they must have felt. How did Moses, Joseph, Simon Peter, John or any of the individuals in the Bible feel about the confusing situation they were walking through? For instance, Moses had no idea GOD would split the Red Sea. He was right in the middle of a confusing situation with GOD. Do you wonder if he was thinking, "OK, here we are. I did exactly what GOD told me to do. For a moment, it looked as if we had escaped. But now, what is this? Why did GOD bring us out here? We could have died in Egypt." And the reason he probably thought those things is the same reason we think those thoughts when our lives are disoriented. We do not know the next step. We do not see how it is all connected. The lack of context is what makes us nervous and afraid. We see it as an isolated event, but we do not see the bigger picture that GOD is painting.

I am reminded of Job from the Old Testament. He was just a normal guy living an ordinary life. He was *"blameless and upright."* Then GOD started bragging on him to satan. From that moment on, everything fell apart. His life turned into a disaster. All his children died. He lost the farm. He came down with a nasty skin disease, and his wife was ready for him to end it all. I have a feeling she had tied a noose in the rope and was handing it to him when she encouraged him *"Curse GOD and die!"* She had had enough. She did not see the bigger picture. But somehow Job did. In Job 19:26-27, he said,

"And after my skin has been destroyed, yet in my flesh I will see GOD. I myself will see Him with my own eyes – I, and not another. How my heart yearns within me!"

In spite of his disorienting season, GOD was still GOD and one day Job would see Him. What Job did not know was that his life would be a central plot in GOD'S story for all of humanity to read, even thousands of years later. Something greater was going on. Although he did not know it, Job was confronting the question that millions have asked ever since: why do bad things happen to good people? His life was connected to every other life.

He Led Them Forth

When life is dark and confusing, remember that GOD'S bigger picture is the truth. Something greater is going on. Your circumstances are connected to the past and the future. Your life is connected to many, many people that you do not even know. GOD is up to something greater. Your role, for the present moment, is to navigate the treacherous path before you. As you walk in GOD'S grace, His plan is carried out and you are better fitted for the destiny He created for you. It's all connected. You just need to back up from the trees to see the forest.

I was inspired by the words of John MacDuff, a Scottish pastor and author from the 1800's. He gives us tremendous insight on the words from Psalm 107:7, KJV:

"And He led them forth by the right way — that they might go to a city of habitation."

God's thoughts are not as our thoughts — neither are His ways as our ways! This truth is strikingly exemplified in the manner in which He led the Israelites from Egypt to the promised land. We would have chosen the way that was nearest and most direct — but God decided otherwise. He led them round about through the wilderness, and that for the space of forty years! And not merely was it the most distant way — but it was the most dangerous way as well. It was a land of deserts and of pits — a land of drought and death — a land that no man passed through, and where no man dwelt.

But, as strange as it appeared, we are fully justified in saying that it was wisely arranged.

Their long detainments;

their tiresome and circuitous wanderings;

their fierce conflicts with the Moabites and the Amalekites;

the bitter waters which they had to drink; and

the fiery serpents with which they were stung —

*all fulfilled the high purposes of Him who is
excellent in counsel, as well as wonderful in
working. However contrary His way might have
been to theirs — yet
"He led them forth by the right way, that they might
go to a city of habitation."*

*And His dealings with His people now, are still
as unusual, and as much opposed to all their
preconceived plans — as were His dealings with the
Israelites! He has crossed their own schemes, and
thwarted their most fondly-cherished purposes! He
always effects His own ends — in His own way!*

*Christian, what is your duty?
It is to cherish high thoughts of God in all His
inscrutable dealings towards you.
It is to trust His heart — even when you can't trace
His hand; believing that "all the paths of the Lord
are mercy and truth, unto such as keep His covenant
and His testimonies."
It is to follow His guidance continually; for as He
led His people of old with "the cloud by day, the
pillared fire by night" — so He has promised to
direct all your steps, and preserve all your goings.
It is to wait His time; for although the way may
appear long and tedious — yet remember, "all is
well, that ends well." And what will the end be?
"And the ransomed of the Lord shall return, and
come to Zion with songs, and everlasting joy upon
their heads! They shall obtain joy and gladness, and
sorrow and sighing shall flee away!"[xv]*

In the midst of our darkness, John MacDuff reminds us
that GOD is accomplishing His plan in ways we could
never imagine. And though the circumstances are
difficult and treacherous, GOD is accomplishing greater

things than we could ever imagine. When you want to question why, then back up from the forest and see the trees. Your life is not your own. Your circumstances are not isolated. They are all connected.

You Must Go Through It

The question that remains to ask is how do we back up from the trees to see the forest? While the question is obvious and simple, the answer is not. I could give you a checklist with things to do like read the Bible, pray, talk to other believers, read biographies, attend worship and Bible study. And all of those actions are encouraged. However, it is difficult, even impossible, to explain your disorientation to someone who has not been through it. A person cannot connect with that kind of situation unless he has walked in those shoes. In other words, I do not think there is a method to accomplish the "backing up to see the forest" process. In fact, I am not sure that GOD will allow us to back up from the trees to see the forest until we are ready to do so. Until we feel the isolation and darkness of that season of life, we cannot know its transforming power. I believe our lostness must be fully experienced for what it is before we can experience His transforming grace. You must go through the forest before you can see it.

In the Bible, Luke tells the story of two eager followers of Jesus traveling to a village called Emmaus immediately after His crucifixion. They were in a season of disorientation. They were feeling the grief of Jesus' horrific crucifixion and death. Their hopes had been dashed. They said, *"We had hoped that He was the one who was going to redeem Israel"* (Luke 24:21). Their darkness and disappointment must have been heavy. It had become apparent that Jesus was not the redeemer they had hoped He would be. And then a stranger came alongside them and started talking to them. He asked them why they were sad. This stranger was actually the resurrected Jesus! They did not know it. In fact, Luke writes that it was not until they stopped for dinner and the stranger, Jesus, blessed their meal that they realized who He was. In his words, *"their eyes were opened"* (Luke 24:31). They could not see the reality of the greater thing GOD was doing because GOD did not want them to see it until the right moment. Part of His plan in our lives is to keep us in darkness until we are ready to receive a greater awareness of the meaning of our darkness. Until we are ready, we will not see it.

But there comes a day when you are able to back up and see it. Not that the questions are answered, but GOD'S purposes are served, your heart is transformed and life is never the same again. You do not even want to go back like you once did. For you have not only embraced the disorientation, you are able to celebrate what GOD has done. Your worship comes from your ability to back up and see the forest. You realize that it's all connected.

Oh the depth of the riches of the wisdom and knowledge of GOD!
How unsearchable His judgments, and His paths beyond tracing out!
Who has known the mind of the Lord?
Or who has been His counselor?
Who has ever given to GOD,
That GOD should ever repay him?
For from Him and through Him and to Him
Are all things.
To Him be the glory forever! Amen!
Romans 11:33-36

Discussion Questions

1. Take time today to look back over your life in "seasons" such as your youth, young adult, middle age, old age. Identify the difficult seasons in those times. What do you remember about them? How did they shape you to become who you are today?

2. Can you identify a bigger work that GOD has been doing? What is the thread that weaves through all of those difficulties?

GOD'S Wonderful Gifts

"In the waiting, we become."
- Jeff Goins[xvi]

Some of God's gifts are simply given. He loves us and often showers us w/ gifts generously. In fact, we were born with some gifts. We only have to discover them.

However some of God's gifts are not given. Rather they are developed. He works in our lives & circumstances to create these gifts. While they are free & in no way earned, neither are they simply handed out. Instead GOD uses the circumstances of life to cause these gifts to well up inside of us, develop & then come forth. These gifts include traits such as courage, compassion, endurance, wisdom and strength. They come forth from the dark times in life when we struggle to face another day. These gifts are the redeeming results of our heartaches.

The words of Hebrews 5:7-8 give me great comfort when I think of my own struggles:

During the days of Jesus' life on earth, He offered up prayers and petitions with fervent cries and tears to the one who could save him from death, and he was heard because of his reverent submission. Son though he was, he learned obedience from what he suffered . . .

Jesus occasionally found Himself crying out to GOD and rather than save Jesus from that dark moment in life, GOD let Him go through it. As a result, Jesus "learned obedience." If I were to guess the most famous people who needed to learn obedience, Jesus would not have been in the top thousand. However, His suffering taught Him obedience.

The Beauty of Our Pain

GOD uses the pressures of life to shape and grow us into the person He created us to be. We see this truth in the common butterfly. Its beauty and strength come from its struggle to escape the cocoon. It must push itself forth. The temptation is to give assistance to the butterfly. And that is also the danger. Only in the pressure of breaking through the wall of the cocoon is the blood and oxygen pushed to the extremities of the wings that enables the butterfly to eventually take flight. Otherwise it is weakened and dies. The butterfly needs the struggle to live. And so do we. Pain can bring profound results.

Consider the words of John Ortberg, pastor of Menlo Park Presbyterian Church:

I once was part of a survey on spiritual formation. Thousands of people were asked when they grew most spiritually, and what contributed to their growth. The response was humbling—at least for someone who works at a church. The number one contributor to spiritual growth was not transformational teaching. It was not being in a small group. It was not reading deep books. It was not energetic worship experiences. It was not finding meaningful ways to serve. It was suffering. People said they grew more during seasons of loss, pain, and crisis than they did at any other time.[xvii]

Pain can be good for us. On the one hand, this thought seems counterintuitive and yet on the other hand, it makes much sense. GOD desires to use our pain to make us more than we are. In those disorienting seasons of life, we are stretched in ways we never imagined. Just like a work-out regimen that presses us to do exercises that tear down our muscles, so the sufferings of this life push us spiritually to depend on GOD. They force us to look heavenward and to listen intently and to respond in ways we don't desire.

They push us emotionally. We are forced to look at our hurts and fears and feelings of despair and ask the question: Why? Why am I feeling these things? What internally is causing me to think like this?

Don't Waste the Struggles

Our challenge is simple: How do we respond to our struggles? My answer is simple: Don't waste them. Don't waste our struggles. If we respond to them with complacency or self-pity, then we have gone nowhere and we have not grown. GOD did not perhaps cause the struggle we face, but He will use it for good if we will respond appropriately.

So you may be wondering if this is simply making lemonade from the lemons. Partially. However, I think that comparing our struggles to lemons is to minimize the struggles that many of us face. The darkness that shrouds our hearts is much more than a sour taste that causes our mouths to wince. A cancer diagnosis, a child's death or a rejected spouse can cause deep sorrow. Therefore, our response of adding a little sugar and water to the situation is not what we need. That response does not cause us or our situation to change. It goes much deeper than that. Change, on GOD'S scale, is beneath the surface. It is at the deep place of the heart. Making lemonade is about making things better, but GOD is about making us better. Disorienting seasons are about GOD growing us & transforming us into individuals we could never become apart from them.

Run to the Darkness

In our moment of darkness, Jerry Sittser encourages us to run to it, not away from it. In 1991, he and his family were traveling home from a family reunion when a drunk driver hit them. His mother, wife and youngest daughter died in the crash. In *A Grace Disguised*, Sittser describes with searing honesty what it was like to be a single father and counselor to others while he himself was a man bereft of hope, slipping into a black hole of oblivion.

One night he had a kind of "waking dream." The sun was setting, and he was frantically chasing after it toward the west, hoping to catch it and bring it back. But it was a losing race. Soon the sun was gone, and he "felt a vast darkness closing in." Shortly after this, his sister Diane told him that the quickest way to reach the sun is not to go west but instead to head east, to move fully "into the darkness until one comes to the sunrise." It was a counterintuitive insight that helped Sittser find a road to recovery:

"I discovered in that moment that I had the power to choose the direction my life would head....I decided from that point on to walk into the darkness rather than try to outrun it, to let my experience of loss take me on a journey wherever it would lead, and to allow myself to be transformed by my suffering rather than to think I could somehow avoid it." [xxviii]

There is no exit strategy when going through a season of lostness. The only response through which GOD works to fulfill His destiny for us is to embrace the experience and walk with Him through it. There is no way around it. Our best attempts to escape will only bring us back around to the same place.

I learned that my focus on getting out of the situation only seemed to compound the darkness. I tended to focus on what I had lost or where I would like to be. I thought a great deal about my failures or mistakes. I complained about the situation a lot. None of those things made a difference. I still was who I was and I still was where I was. Once I embraced the reality that GOD was at work in my moment of lostness, I was able to move forward. No longer did the doubts and anger and disappointment hound me day after day. I was not completely finished with those companions, but they did not chase me as much. Once I was able to look inside and ask GOD what He wanted me to see in my own heart, I was able to recognize the positive difference the silent darkness was making. I saw how I was growing. The transforming work of the Holy Spirit was evident to me. As a result, it comforted me to know that GOD had not disqualified me from leadership. Rather it meant that He had much more work to do through me and therefore He had much work to do in me. In the words of Joseph, I too realized that GOD intended it for good (Genesis 50:20).

One of the good gifts GOD was developing was wisdom. James, the half-brother of Jesus, made the connection between difficult seasons of life and the gaining of wisdom. In the New Testament (James 1:4-5), he wrote:

Let perseverance finish its work so that you may be mature and complete, not lacking anything. If any of you lacks wisdom, you should ask GOD, who gives generously to all without finding fault, and it will be given to you.

We gain wisdom when we are called on to persevere. Wisdom is not a gift that GOD simply hands over to us. Wisdom is an ability that GOD develops in us when we are challenged. We learn lessons about ourselves, about Him and about life that last us a lifetime. The difficulties of life teach us the ways of GOD. They show us the depths of our own hearts. And sometimes we begin to see others more clearly as well. Isn't that the essence of wisdom? So as we press on during the struggles we face, one of our primary prayers should be for wisdom because that is one of GOD'S greatest desires for us, to gain a heart of wisdom.

A Greater Capacity

I realized that GOD was developing a greater capacity in me during this time. Throughout my life, I have felt as if there was something more out there. Words defy my ability to explain that statement. But something in my heart has kept telling me over the years that I was not living out of the full potential of GOD'S calling. And I wondered why. I remember the frustrations I had with the congregations I pastored. My prayers were focused on GOD doing something powerful in their lives. But now I realize that my frustrations were really about me, not them. They were not the ones at fault. I was. I did not possess the capacity to lead them further. GOD wanted to do more, but my heart could only hold a certain amount of all that

GOD was pouring into it. I needed a "capacity increase." As I look back now at my lostness, I realize that is what GOD was doing. He was increasing my capacity. He was giving me a deeper heart.

When I was training to run a marathon, I would run a little further each week. I ran two miles the first week. I ran three miles the next week. Then I ran five miles, then seven miles and so on. I was increasing my capacity to run further. I was training my legs and lungs and heart and every part of my body to run twenty-six miles. Even my toes were in training. I was increasing my capacity to do something I had never done before. I was thankful that GOD was taking me to places to do things I had never done before. He was increasing my capacity.

The prayer of Ephesians 3:20 became my heartcry. It is there we read that GOD is:

". . . able to do immeasurably more than all we ask or imagine according to His power that is at work within us.

I began praying that GOD would do immeasurably more in me so that He could do immeasurably more through me. I did not want my lack of capacity to hinder the greatness of His desires to impact the people that He had placed around me.

While I took great comfort in this thought, I also understood why I felt disoriented. GOD was working in my life in ways that I could not understand. He was doing more than my mind could even imagine. It was beyond my ability to comprehend what GOD was accomplishing. I could not grasp the depth of His immeasurable work in me. So when I would ask why this was happening, the silence meant that my mind could not grasp what He was doing so there was nothing He could say. All I could do was trust Him.

This wisdom was so transforming to me. The ways of GOD are too great for us to imagine sometimes. So we should not be surprised when we do not comprehend His plans and purposes. Those moments are the times we should realize that the darkness clearly reveals light.

These disorienting seasons are about the work GOD wants to do in us and they are also about the work that GOD wants to do through us. We do not want to miss out on that.

Discussion Questions

1. Pain has transforming power because it gets down to the depths of our soul.

What are the valuable lessons pain has taught you?

2. What are the beautiful results that have come out of your trials?

3. If you have experienced the death of a vision in your life, it may mean you were not ready for the vision. Is your vision greater than you? How do you see GOD developing a greater internal capacity?

The Day When Things Went Dark
Bruce Pittman

Do you remember the day when things went dark?
Do you remember trying to find your way without any
light?
Do you remember the feeling of lostness?
Never having walked this way before.

We had never been left out in the cold.
But we were on this day.
The day when things went dark.

We could barely look at each other.
New emotions arose inside.
We knew not what to do.
When things go dark, life is different.

Sadness
Shame
Uncertainty
Fear
Anger
Darkness

"Quiet! Listen! Do you hear?
Quick! Over there! Hide! He's coming!"
How do you hide from searching love?
It stops at nothing until it finds its desire.
The beckoning of His voice drew us out,
    "Where are you?"

Darkness hid from the light.
"We were afraid. We were ashamed."
    "Who told you?"

Pointing fingers replaced arms of embrace.
Names were condemned.
Blame was shouted.
Curses defined us.

A sacrifice was paid.
Blood flowed.
A covering was made.

In another moment of darkness –
    "Father, forgive them." Light!

A Wilderness of My Own Choosing

"Lord, is it me? What have I done? Search my heart. Know me. Try my thoughts. See if there is any wicked way in me." I prayed those words from Psalm 139 many times during my lostness. GOD was silent and I wondered often if and how I had offended Him. The very last thing I desired was distance from Him. If I had misinterpreted His plan and failed to obey Him, then I was ready to repent.

One issue that came to my mind when I would pray this prayer was related to church planting. My failure to maintain boundaries during that time stole my joy. I was working each and every day to birth this church. I did not honor the Sabbath like GOD had told me to do. Before long, that flame burned out. I learned from that mistake. GOD is not honored by people who work with no rest. I realized that my failure to observe the Sabbath meant I was trusting my effort rather than GOD'S power. I was living impatiently rather than waiting on GOD. My agenda had taken precedence over His. I repented.

What Jonah Would Tell Us

Occasionally, we end up in the wilderness of lostness because of our sinful choices. That was the story of the Exodus. When the Israelite people left Egypt, the land of GOD'S promise was only a journey of a few days. Yet their rebellion against GOD extended their journey in the wilderness into forty years!

The Old Testament tells the story of a guy named Jonah. GOD had a plan for Jonah to go to a city called Nineveh. The Lord was deeply concerned about their sinful choices so He wanted Jonah to instruct them to turn away from their lifestyle. The only problem with this plan was that Jonah did not appreciate GOD'S desire to forgive Nineveh. He chose to disobey. Jonah booked a Mediterranean cruise to Tarshish, the opposite direction of Nineveh. His beautiful trip became a disaster. A massive storm arose during his excursion. Jonah knew what was going on. He knew that his disobedience was the cause of the storm. He asked the sailors to throw him overboard. I guess he was too afraid to jump in on his own. Although the sailors did not want to do so, they did as he asked and the storm immediately stopped. A giant fish swimming nearby gulped Jonah down. For three days, Jonah survived the belly of the fish. During that time, he came to his senses and repented. His prayer was, *"What I have vowed, I will make good."* The fish became nauseous and vomited Jonah on the beach. That experience must have been horribly gross. However, the result is that Jonah *"obeyed the word of the Lord and went to Nineveh."*

Jonah experienced the discipline of GOD because he was disobedient. Although he knew clearly what GOD wanted him to do, he refused to do it. Jonah intentionally ran the other direction of GOD'S will. He was punished. He landed in the stomach of the fish for several days. When he repented, GOD released him from the fish. He then went and obeyed GOD.

The message of Jonah is clear. When we disobey GOD, the consequences are certain to come. GOD's punishment is designed to show us the error of our ways and to bring us to the place where we will obey Him – even unwillingly as Jonah did.

The Good Results of Discipline

Those moments of sin will bring on GOD'S discipline in the same way. However, His discipline is not designed just to punish us. Rather, His discipline is designed to grow us. I remember the times my parents disciplined me. At the core, it was an alignment problem. Let me explain. I had ideas about what I wanted to do with my time and none of them were related to doing my chores. However, my parents also had ideas about my time and my chores. My thinking and their thinking were not aligned. They were thinking one way and I was thinking another way. In order to communicate clearly that it was their way or no way, they needed to discipline me. Their goal was not to hurt me. Their goal was to change the way I thought. I needed to learn the significance of aligning the way I thought with the way that they thought. Otherwise, I would have an alignment problem for the rest of my life.

Another issue related to discipline is clarity. Jonah needed to realize that GOD was not giving him an option. GOD was not looking for a volunteer. GOD was not suggesting that Jonah change his plans for the future. GOD was commanding Jonah to go to Nineveh. He needed clarity that GOD was not giving him a suggestion. The storm and the fish did the trick. Jonah understood.

The power of GOD'S discipline is that He changes the way we think. We get alignment and we get clarity. We learn to live in obedience. If we are naturally stubborn, the discipline may take more than one experience. Like a parent who deeply loves His child, GOD will keep on pursuing us as an expression of His love. His continuing discipline is a continuing reminder that He has not let us go in a direction that will eventually destroy us.

We Must Grow Up

Jesus does set us free from the bondage of sin. His presence in our lives gives us the ability to choose to do the right thing. However, we must grow up at some point and begin to do the right thing. We may be free from sin, but that freedom does not automatically guarantee that we will not go back to it. It is comparable to the parents of a growing infant. That child will regularly wet his diaper and will need it changed and the parents will do that gladly until he knows better. However, the day comes when the kid needs to grow up and stop wetting his pants. In the same way, Jesus will take care of our messes, but somewhere down the road we need to grow up and stop making messes. His discipline is designed to clarify and align us to the fact that we are making messes because like Jonah, we are choosing to disobey Him and go our direction.

Occasionally we end up lost not because we are following Jesus, but because we are not following Jesus. So if you feel lost, a critical question to ask is: am I headed to Tarshish when I should be going to Nineveh? Always ask the question of repentance. Perhaps something inside is broken that has been hidden from your sight. Only GOD has seen it. He has brought you to this moment of lostness in order to get your attention. Discipline does that. If it is disobedience, take the road of repentance. Turn around.

"Come, let us return to the Lord. He has torn us to pieces but He will heal us;
He has injured us but He will bind up our wounds.
After two days He will revive us; on the third day He will restore us, that we may live in his presence.
Let us acknowledge the Lord; let us press on to acknowledge Him.

As surely as the sun rises, He will appear;
He will come to us like the winter rains, like the spring
rains that water the earth."
- Hosea 6:1-3

Discussion Questions

1. Repentance means a change of mind. It is not a once in a lifetime event, but rather a continual transformation. How do you experience continuous transformation?

2. Name some areas in your life where you have changed your thinking over the past year.

3. Describe a time in your life when you experienced GOD'S willingness to forgive you, heal you and restore you.

What's Your Name?

In ancient times and cultures children were named for a purpose. Their names were not chosen because of the way they sounded or because they were popular. Parents would name their children based on what they envisioned for them. A name had significance. It often revealed their character or the character their parents desired. It was their true identity.

For instance, in the Bible the name Samuel meant "asked of GOD." Jacob meant "trickster." Israel meant "GOD rules." Joshua meant "The Lord saves." The name revealed the heart.

In Exodus 3, GOD spoke to Moses through a burning bush. GOD was calling Moses to lead the Hebrew slaves out of Egypt to the land of freedom. Assuming the Hebrew slaves would doubt his experience, he asked GOD what His name was. They wanted to know this GOD who had sent Moses to rescue them. So they asked for His name

GOD'S clarifying response was not so clarifying.

God said to Moses, "I AM WHO I AM. This is what you are to say to the Israelites:
'I AM has sent me to you.' God also said to Moses, "Say to the Israelites, 'The Lord, the God of your fathers—the God of Abraham, the God of Isaac and the God of Jacob—has sent me to you.' This is my name forever, the name by
which I am to be remembered from generation to generation.
- Exodus 3:14-15

"I am who I am" was the God who was rescuing them. That was His name. What did that mean? It identified Him to be there in their present, not yesterday, not tomorrow, but today. He would be there with them wherever and whenever they were. He had been there with them in their days of idolatry and slavery. And now the Lord would be with them to liberate them from Pharaoh with amazing wonders. He would be there as they journeyed through the wilderness times of idolatry and lostness. He would be an ever-present GOD. He proved that His name was His character.

What's Your Name?

What about you? What is your name? Who are you? Do you know how to name yourself? Do you know your heart? Is it a name you are willing to share?

Who wants to be known? In reality, everyone does. The heaviness of hiding the real heart is burdensome and yet no one wants to be known. Revealing one's heart is often a journey of trepidation and fear. After all, how will others think of me if they find out the real me and my real name?

I struggled with being known. I was unsure how known I wanted to be. I was concerned about the reactions of others to my personal story becoming public. In the initial efforts to put my story in writing, Kim, my wife read some of it and said that it just did seem to connect. As I re-read the material, I noticed my pattern of using the pronoun "we" instead of "I". In this, I realized that I was having a difficult time of owning my journey. I kept pushing it away even when writing about it. But once I made it mine, the message became powerful and compelling and Kim noticed the difference. Ownership of one's failures makes it authentic. Authenticity gives authority. It means the words are not meaningless; rather, they are full of passion and significance. The shared story means that it matters. When you share your story, you share your identity. You share your name.

Sharing Your Name

John Townsend wrote, *"The more known we are, the more healed we are."*[xix] Secrets have a powerful place in a heart. Like a lie, they take on a life of their own. They have the power to control us. However, when that secret is revealed, its power is gone. Freedom reigns.

A person with no meaningful relationships has many secrets. He has no one he can trust so he keeps his secrets to himself. It is in the context of trusted friends that secrets can be revealed and people can live in freedom. In that freedom is healing – from shame, fear and despair. Everyone needs a place to tell his name and to tell his story. Isn't that the way that Alcoholics Anonymous meetings work? Don't they begin with introductions? "Hi. My name is Bruce. I am an alcoholic." You share your name. You share your story and it is safe place to do that. Secrets are revealed. People begin the path toward freedom when they tell their name.

My journey involved a network of people I learned to trust. Church planting taught me the enormous value of relationships. I have regularly met with different groups of guys and individuals on a regular basis for several years now. They have been a lifesaver for me in many ways. I have been able to be authentic with them with no need to guard my words. They have given me a safe place to be real. I am grateful for it.

Who I Am

Perhaps you are wondering about my name? I look back over the time I have been following Jesus and I see how different seasons of life were moments that my name changed. For instance, my graduation from seminary was a season when I was "Pride." A difficult season followed where I knew myself as "Humbled." I experienced a season of life where I was "Thirsty." I can also recall a time when I was "Spoiled." Perhaps you are asking what my name is now. At this point, I believe I see myself as "Sustained." GOD has taught me and enabled me to press on. I have lived in the strength of His grace to get up every morning and take another step in the direction of His calling. He has sustained my faith, my hope, my joy, my love. He has sustained me. When I wanted to quit, He called for me. When I looked for an exit, He shut the doors. When I tried to run, He surrounded me. When I tried to hide, He searched for me. When I fell, He caught me. When I complained, He listened. When I wanted answers, He kept silent. In every moment of this season of lostness, He has sustained me and in the process enabled me to endure and press on. My journey is not over. A long road awaits me. GOD continues to transform me so that one day I will celebrate His grace that enabled me to overcome the trials of this life. The reason I know that is because of His words about a new name when I finish this race.

"To the one who is victorious, I will give some of the hidden manna. I will also give that person a white stone with a new name written on it, known only to the one who receives it."
Revelation 2:17

Discussion Questions

1. Have you ever looked up the meaning of your name? Were you named after someone?
What did you discover?

2. We need to keep certain areas of our lives private. However there are things we need to share with at least one person. Do you have someone you can share secrets with? How has being known helped you to heal and become stronger?

3. What is your name today? Who is GOD making you to become?

A New Kind of Normal
Carol Kent[xx]

When despair tries to take me under…I choose life.

When I wonder what God could possibly be thinking…
I choose trust.

When I desperately want relief from unrelenting
reality…
I choose perseverance.

When I feel oppressed by my disappointment and
sorrow…I choose gratitude.

When I want to keep my feelings to myself…I choose
vulnerability.

When nothing goes according to my plan…I choose
relinquishment.

When I want to point the finger…I choose forgiveness.

When I want to give up…I choose purposeful action.

Leading from a True Heart

Woman falls off tall white horse and hits the ground hard. Over time, she heals and takes her place in the real world. Although her gift is small, she has the gift of helping people see their unique talent. She seeks out people in pain—excluded, stuck, certain life has passed them by or beset with loss—to whom she may give her gift.[xxi]

-Gloria Rose

At one time, her life, though not perfect, was one that many people would desire, and then one day, it all fell apart. In her own words, she wrote: *" . . . Everything crashed. A move ended the job. Husband walked out. Teenaged children left home. For the first time I knew pain, suffering, and bewilderment. Interestingly, bereft of others' stories, I found mine."* She found herself in the darkness. She found her story in the darkness. Her parable is my parable and it is yours most likely. It is the discovery of our hearts.

Leadership and Self-Awareness

Self-awareness lies at the heart of healthy leadership. LaRae Quy is a former FBI agent who spent 24 years as an undercover agent. She is a motivational speaker and author of *Secrets of a Strong Mind*. In her blog, she wrote:

Leadership begins with knowing who we are and what we believe. Authenticity is the need for leaders to be

*themselves regardless
of the situation. For this reason, it is more than self-
awareness; it is the ability to share the deepest and
truest part of ourselves with others. Leadership begins
with knowing who we are and what we believe.
Authenticity is the need for leaders to be themselves
regardless of the situation. For this reason, it is more
than self-awareness; it is the ability to share the deepest
and truest part of ourselves with others.*[xxii]

As a leader, I have watched other leaders. I have noticed that among the many differences between healthy and unhealthy leaders, one critical issue is self-awareness. Healthy leaders know who they are. They have looked into their own hearts. They know what is going on inside. Unhealthy leaders, however, seem to be unaware of what is going on inside. They don't see the weaknesses, tendencies or structure of a false-self that is built on the foundation of sand.

As a result, the things they build do not last because they built them out of self-ignorance, not self-knowledge. This lack of knowledge is one reason they make bad choices that lead them down roads to moral failure, marriage disintegration, career flops and financial disasters. They are trying to become someone, but they are not sure who that person is or what that person does. Since they do not know who they are, they do not know what to do. The structures they build with their lives fall because they are built on unknown foundations.

The Leadership Trap of Comparison
Self-awareness was the major difference in me before my lostness and after my lostness. As I reflect on

the early days of my leadership, I remember trying to force things to work. I looked for programs that succeeded at other churches. I remember comparing myself with other pastors and other churches. I remember measuring success by numbers and getting stressed out when I was not measuring up to whatever numerical standard I had set up. I was very spiritual about this, too. I remember extended times of prayer asking GOD to do something marvelous in our lives and in the church. I fervently looked and hoped for His power to be revealed. I felt that if I prayed more, then He would answer my prayers. But He didn't, at least not in the ways I desired.

It was a very stressful time, but I thought that was normal for a pastor because that is what I heard other pastors say. While leadership is stressful to some degree, I realized that the stress I was feeling was internal. It was the stress of trying to figure out my own heart. I did not know who I was or what I was supposed to do. All I knew was that I was not doing enough and neither was GOD. While I believed that the extended times of prayer and fasting were a driving passion for Him, I wonder now if they were not expressions of a self-imposed stress. I wanted to be more. I wanted to do more. Yet I did not understand why it was not happening. I was frustrated. My leadership was not working as I thought it should. I even remember moments of thinking about doing something else besides lead. I felt as if I were failing and was tired of the stress. I wanted it to be easier. GOD was making me into a leader, but I wanted to be something else.

I Am the Problem

I can also look back now and see the walls of isolation I had built. The blocks of fear, people pleasing and uncertainty had isolated my heart, keeping it hidden from others and even from myself. I thought that was the way it was supposed to be because that was how I saw other leaders. No one told me about mentoring. No one talked about transparent leadership or being an authentic leader. Even though I participated in a weekly meeting of a small group of pastors, I did not share much of my heart with them because I did not know my heart.

Over a period of two years, I came to the conclusion that the main issue in our church (and in most churches) was a structural problem. We were not structured to reach out to people and to meet them where they were. We were structured with programs that spoke our language and met our needs. We expected outsiders, the people we thought we desperately wanted to reach, to meet us where we were. We were not set up to meet them at their point of need nor did we speak their language. This realization was a major contributing factor to our moving to plant a church. I felt that creating an externally oriented focus would build a structure that would create open doors for people outside the church. And I was right. The church we started was a beginning place for many unchurched people. A large percentage of those who began attending did not come from other churches. However, the problem that remained was my own heart.

Although I had found the right environment in the church plant, GOD still had to do a work in me. He had to show me my heart, tear down its structure, rip up the false foundation, and then restructure it into something deep and real. He needed to take me on a journey to the inner room of my own heart. So He called me away from church and vocational ministry for more than five years so that I could see who He was making me. At the end of that journey I was able to accept who I was and gained a great confidence in who GOD was making me. I realized that I was becoming more. I knew that GOD was fulfilling His destiny for my life. I was living on purpose and direction. I had a calling to pursue. It narrowed the focus of my life. I was no longer trying to become someone because I knew who I was. I was able to live and to lead securely from my true self, not from false self. I willingly took on the leadership mantle GOD had been reserving for me. This was who I was; I knew it and I was ready for the new adventures that awaited me.

What a Leader Really Needs to Know

Self-awareness is the anchor that holds a leader in place so she can launch into a specific direction with confidence. She does not fear the waves of the sea or the winds of the air that can take her off course or wreck her life. She is ready and able to do battle with the forces that come against her. She knows where she has been, what GOD is making her and where He is leading her. This assurance is the pad off which a leader can launch into the future.

John Holm is a consulting coach for individuals and teams who are in the process of transformational leadership. He wrote:

What is needed in every great leader is for the leader to be "well-defined." I've rarely coached someone who decided that more knowledge or more skill would help them become a successful leader Instead, what they needed to learn was more about themselves.

A well-defined leader is one who is internally aligned. What they say complements what they do. It looks like this:

1. Their thinking rules over their emotions.

2. They're a non-anxious presence.

3. They have firm, appropriate boundaries.

4. They have clarity of self and their own goals.

5. They consider self when problems arise.

6. They welcome conflict that is centered on mission.

7. They know their own core values and live them out in actions.

Think of a leader you respect and would love to learn from. They most likely fit the description above.[xxiii]

Only as I lead myself am I able to lead others.

On the night of His betrayal, Jesus had this same confidence. He was facing the torture of his arrest, trial and ultimate crucifixion, and yet He was able to disrobe, pick up a towel and washbasin, and wash the feet of His followers. Where did He find this assurance to humble Himself? I would have been a nervous wreck anticipating such a horrific future. Read John's words.

Jesus knew that the Father had put all things under His power, and that He had come from God and was returning to GOD; So he got up from the meal, took off His outer clothing, and wrapped a towel around His waist. After that, He poured water into a basin and began to wash His disciples' feet, drying them with the towel that was wrapped around Him.
John 13:3-5

Jesus was able to follow His Father's direction because of His self-awareness. He knew who He was and where He was going. He could do so with confidence and courage. He had no second guessing. He did not hesitate. Jesus stepped into the future and changed the world.

Self-aware leaders know what they were made to do and they do it. They do not look to do something else other than what they are made and gifted to do. They do it with passion and joy and success. Great results come when leaders do what GOD made them to do.

The Confidence of Self-Awareness

These leaders lead people to do more and to be more. Isn't that the essence of leadership - Guiding people on a path toward GOD'S destiny for them? Aren't leaders the ones who inspire, encourage and instruct others to be more than they are? The leaders who lead people to do and to be more are leaders who have become more themselves. They have gotten in touch with their heart, they know who God made them to be and they lead out of that authentic heart. They have gone through that season of darkness and have come out on the other side with a clear heart and a defined vision. Rather than lead from a perceived personality, they lead from the essence of who they are. They are not trying to impress anyone or win approval or keep people happy. They do not lead from fear or from false impressions or from pleasing others. They are not threatened by the controlling personalities of others. They solve problems based on logical and clear answers, not based on politics. They are comfortable with the reality that although they are more than they were, they are still a work in progress along with everyone else.

They exude confidence, but not cockiness. They can lead others into an uncertain future because of the certainty of who they are. They have focus and direction. They are stable. They know, above all else, that they too are followers. The path they travel has the unmistakable footprints of Jesus in the dust. These leaders know who they are, whose they are and where they are going. These leaders are the leaders we all want to become.

Discussion Questions

1. If leadership is influence, do you see yourself as a leader?

If so, how have you seen your influence grow due to your self-discovery?

2. Do you regularly compare yourself to others (perhaps unknowingly)?

Name specific areas where you don't feel confident in your own skin.

3. John Holm wrote that leaders become more successful because of what they learn about themselves. What have you learned about yourself in the reading of this book?

The Thing Before Us

During this period of darkness when we had no direction, one of the many important lessons that took root in our hearts was that the waiting time is not always a place to do nothing. Sometimes waiting is a moment to do something. While GOD occasionally sets us aside to rest and recover, especially if we refuse to do that on our own, there are times when GOD sets us aside to do something productive. Once we felt some wind in our sails and were feeling restless and ready to go, we fell on a simple principle that really changed our lives. It had started earlier in our married lives.

See the Need; Meet the Need

One day I was whining about something trivial that needed attention like an overflowing laundry basket. I made a sarcastic remark like, "well, it looks like it is time for the laundry lady to get to work." My wife quickly responded, "See the need. Meet the need." Later that day, I was able to watch the ball game while I folded the clothes I had washed and dried.

That simple principle took root in our hearts and we began to live it out. We phrased it differently: Do the thing before you. We started doing just that. Rather than wringing our hands trying to figure out what GOD was calling us to do (although we certainly did that), we decided to live this simple principle.

We saw needs all around us, just a step outside of our door. We decided to meet those needs. We did the things before us. Instead of looking for something to do, we just opened our eyes to the world around us and stepped into it. We had no need to search for some way to serve GOD. There was no reason to go on a mission trip. We just got up each morning and looked before us. The opportunities to serve Him were abundant. Many of them were simple and small. Some were significant. Some of them were financial. All of them cost us time. A sacrifice of some sort was always involved, but time was abundant for us during this season. If GOD was willing to lay us aside for that season in life, then why should we be in a hurry? So we began to spend our time wisely by investing it in others.

We cut our neighbors' grass when they were called out of town unexpectedly with a medical emergency. We helped a friend who was trying to get sober. We painted and reinstalled the shutters of an elderly friend who had taken the initiative to take them down himself. We spent time with a friend going through a divorce. We bought beds for children whose mother had died. We sponsored missionaries and church planters. We assisted friends who were moving. We bought dinner and paid for a motel room one Christmas Eve for a homeless woman. We discovered people all around us who needed inspiration, friendship, support, laughter and hope. Some of them were strangers. Many were neighbors, friends and family. We had listening ears, strong backs, generous hands and willing hearts. GOD gave us the grace to see needs as opportunities to be the hands and feet of Jesus in our everyday, ordinary world, and He gave us the desire to meet those needs.

Don't Forget People

Perhaps the most surprising way we served others was by not dropping them after their crisis was over. When you do something for someone, it is easy to do what that person needs and then move on. However, we realized the importance of staying with people after the need was met. We learned not to drop people after their crisis was over. We would often follow up later with a phone call, text or email and ask the question, "How's it going?" The reason it was so powerful was because it communicated that their need was not another mission accomplished. Rather, it said to them that they were the focus of our concern, not just their need. They mattered.

Were these things I wanted to do? Not always. Were they the desires of my heart? Not completely. Did I want to spend a lifetime doing these kinds of things? No. I knew that GOD had made me and had called me to something else. However, my wife and I decided that we could not just sit back and do nothing. We decided to serve Jesus in small ways by doing the thing before us. Did we serve everyone we met? No. In fact, I must confess that we passed up opportunities to serve others generously on numerous occasions. I distinctly remember a trip through South Carolina. We encountered a lady at a gas station whose battery had gone dead. She was waiting on someone with jumper cables. We had no jumper cables and could not help. After driving away, I said to my family, "Well I guess we should have bought her a battery." But it was too late.

Serving Others Is Healing

Do you know what we discovered in these small acts of kindness? We discovered joy. In the midst of our darkness, we found light by looking beyond ourselves and our own needs and investing in others. While we could not affect our own situation regardless of how hard we tried, we could affect the situations of others. So we did. We stepped into their circumstances and did what we could to make a difference. And those moments of serving others were moments of satisfaction. We enjoyed being the answers to their prayers. GOD met their needs through us and that experience was fulfilling to us. We helped other people get where they needed to go and we counted those opportunities as privileges. Things changed for others because GOD prompted us to step in and make a difference and in the process we changed. We experienced joy because of the needs of others.

Researchers have discovered that helping others is a great benefit to people who suffer from depression.

They found that "positive activity interventions" -- like helping someone with groceries,   writing a thank you note or even counting your blessings -- can serve as an effective, low-   cost treatment for depression.

"They seem really trivial. They seem like, what's the big deal, you feel good for 10 minutes," said Sonja Lyubomirsky, a psychology professor at the University of California, Riverside, who co-authored a recent paper on the topic. "But for a depressed person, they aren't trivial at all. Depressed individuals need to increase positive emotions in their life, even a minute here and there."

After a rigorous review of research on the therapeutic benefits of positive emotion, Lyubomirsky said, she and her colleagues found widespread support for the notion that   people with a tendency toward depression can help themselves by helping others or otherwise introducing positivity into their day-to-day lives.[xxiv]

GOD created us with a built-in means of bringing light to our dark place of depression. It is called meeting the needs of others. When we care for others, it does something for us. It is the connection that Jesus made when He said to love our neighbor as we love ourselves. When we reach out to others, something therapeutic happens inside of us.

Is that not what the Lord was declaring in Isaiah 58:6-9?

"Is not this the kind of fasting I have chosen:
to loose the chains of injustice and untie the cords of
the yoke, to set the oppressed free and break every yoke?
Is it not to share your food with the hungry and to
provide the poor wanderer with shelter— when you see
the naked, to clothe him, and not to turn away from your
own flesh and blood? Then your light will break forth
like the dawn, and your healing will quickly appear;
then your righteousness will go before you, and the
glory of the Lord will be your rear guard. Then you will
call, and the Lord will answer; you will cry for help, and
he will say: Here am I.

When we choose to serve others rather than focus on ourselves, His light will shine into our darkness and bring healing to our brokenness. His presence becomes evident.

Just Show Up and See What Happens

GOD was doing something new in the depths of our hearts. He was teaching us about more than serving. He was creating a servant's heart inside of us. We had willingly served others before, but during this time, serving and giving became intuitive to us. The "see the need, meet the need" reaction became automatic. We began to think like that. We did the thing before us. We looked for ways to be generous. We asked about opportunities to give money to others rather than shy away from them. And it was not because we felt guilty about having something that others did not have. We were not motivated by guilt. It was genuine compassion that moved us to serve and give. GOD was teaching us the power and joy of giving away our lives & living as though we were not our own. We were learning to live for the sake of other people around us.

It was during this season that I began most every day with this prayer:

Today Jesus will You . . .

Give me Your eyes to see what You see.
Give me Your ears to hear what You hear.
Give me Your hands to do what You do.
Give me Your feet to go where You go.
Give me Your mind to think what You think.
Give me Your heart to want what You want.
Give me Your mouth to say what You say.

Because it is no longer I who live, but it is You who lives in me.

We were seeing the words of Ephesians 2:10 come alive for us:

For we are GOD'S handiwork, created in Christ Jesus to do good works, which GOD prepared in advance for us to do.

The things we were doing were ordained by GOD. It was not of our own planning, but it was of His divine design for us. GOD had opportunities waiting on us every morning. Each day was another chance to serve Him by serving others. He was putting people and situations before us, so we did what was before us.

During this season of disorientation, we were praying, "GOD, what do You want us to do? Open a door for us Lord!" and then we would look up and see a need. He did just as we asked. He opened a door. It was not the door we envisioned or the door we desired. But how could we walk away from it just because we did not want to do it? We were learning that a servant's heart does not pick and choose where or when he serves. He does what is before him.

It Starts at Home

We experienced this in no better place than our own home. We were learning to serve each other as well. When times were tough, we came to the realization that we all were doing all we knew to do. The disastrous season was not because anyone had made bad decisions or because anyone was being foolish. We had gotten there because of our sincere desire to follow Jesus. Rather than get angry with each other, which is often typical for families in stress, we simply stepped up our game and gave ourselves away to each other. We did not complain about shoes being left on the floor or forgotten items at school or a misplaced remote or not having enough money. Whether it was due to laziness or forgetfulness, we operated with the assumption that everybody was doing their best. We stopped asking the selfish questions about what we wanted and started asking the serving questions about what we could do. Serving others became a core value for our family.

As a result, GOD did shine His light into our darkness. We had joy. We felt encouraged. GOD was using us to impact lives. We were giving hope to people in small ways and as a result, we were feeling that hope in our own hearts. Regardless of the negative feelings and the disparaging voices, we would find ourselves coming back around to a heart of joy. That joy made all the difference to us in our home when we felt lost and unsure.

Discussion Questions

1. While you are reading this book about your own heart, stop for a moment and ask yourself: What are the needs right around me? Whose life could I touch in the next 24 hours that would make an enormous difference?

2. What attitudes hinder you from serving others?

3. Why can it be easier to buy a homeless guy a meal than it is to pick up our spouse's socks?

Prepare the Way

It was early in the church planting experience that my wife and I were sitting at a busy intersection waiting for the traffic light to turn green. We were discussing the process and how it had been a very different time in our lives. As we talked, my wife made an insightful statement. "I believe this is more about our boys than it is us."

We have often looked back on that unforgettable moment of clarity because it has proven to be true on many levels. During this challenging time, we had numerous conversations with our children about the difficulties and doubts of what we were enduring. Together we talked about the deeper issues of our hearts such as the disappointments and the need for patience. Our family talked about the struggle to trust that GOD was working in spite of our circumstances. Rather than shy away from the difficult realities of walking with GOD, we discussed them openly and frequently with our sons. More and more we realized that it was more about our boys than it was us." GOD was working in their lives for a prosperous and hopeful future. His plans involved the planting of this church and so much more. He was putting steel in their faith at an early age.

It was a parenting lesson for us and a lesson for everyone who answers to the name of mom or dad. When life is hard and your faith is being tested, do not ignore the children. Let them be as much a part of the challenge as they can. Do not shield them from the difficulty of serving a GOD who does things we cannot understand. It is in those moments of darkness that children begin to see most clearly with eyes of faith and learn to hold His hand in the dark. Let them walk with you through it.

Prepare the Way for Them

A mistake I see parents make is being short-sighted. We tend to think in terms of the segments of our children's lives. Often our goal is to get them potty trained or to finish the fifth grade or to graduate from high school or to get a job. On some days, I know that the small victories really count, especially potty training. However, we can fail to look at the long road and the big picture. Perhaps one day your children will have the opportunity to look back on their lives and evaluate them. What is it you want them to see? To think? To feel? Most of us answer with words like content, satisfied, joyous, grateful or fulfilled. Now ask yourself: what is it you can do for them now that will be a step in that direction? How can you prepare the way for them to get there? How can you set them up for this kind of success?

You may be thinking that it is too late. Your child may be in college or at mid-life or later. The good news is that it is not too late. It is rarely too late for parents to invest more in their children. It is rarely too late to have a meaningful conversation. It is rarely too late to open up about the past. It is rarely too late to ask for forgiveness. Our children have a lot of road to travel between now and then. To get there, they need their parents to look ahead of them and prepare the way.

GOD Has a Destiny

What do you see when you look at your child? Do you see destiny written over him or her? You should because that is how and why GOD created that child.

He had a specific purpose when He formed him/her in the womb. We as parents have the awesome privilege to partner with GOD in preparing them for His purpose. The task for every parent is to help their children discover their destiny. King David, a man of destiny himself, wrote this poem to GOD (Psalm 139, Message):

> *Oh yes, You shaped me first inside, then out; You formed me in my mother's womb.*
> *I thank you, High God—you're breathtaking!*
>   *Body and soul, I am marvelously made!*
>   *I worship in adoration—what a creation!*
> *You know me inside and out, You know every bone in my body;*
> *You know exactly how I was made, bit by bit, how I was sculpted from nothing into something.*
> *Like an open book, you watched me grow from conception to birth;*
> *All the stages of my life were spread out before you,*
> *The days of my life all prepared before I'd even lived one day.*

In a sentence, every single life was created for a divine purpose. No child was haphazardly birthed. Destiny is not something that comes to us, but rather it is something within us. Destiny is who we are, not what we do, because in the words of David, "You shaped me."

It is a tragic experience when parents forget this. But how often have parents walked out of a school or jail or hospital disappointed and disheartened at where their son or daughter is sleeping that night? It is easy to lose sight of this truth when our children make wrong choices that land them in a bad situation. So we parents must constantly remember that regardless of what they choose to do in those reckless moments, GOD still has a destiny for them.

Tell Them

Make sure your children understand that GOD has a destiny for them. Clearly and repeatedly communicate to them that GOD has called them. Calling is not just about ministers or pastors. Calling is about embracing GOD'S plan regardless of its being vocational ministry. Every follower of Jesus is a minister. Sometimes those ministers wear gym shorts on a basketball court or a dress suit in a court room. You will see His destiny unfold for them. It will happen as you tell them from early on that this great GOD of the universe has planned a future for them to discover and fulfill. There should never be a day in a child's life that he doesn't know he is living out GOD'S destiny for his lives.

Help them to understand the vastness of His call. Some may object and say that all of this talk about "destiny" will make them proud. Actually it will do the opposite. As they begin to grasp the expanse of His calling, it will humble them to a place of utter dependence on GOD to fulfill His destiny. As dads tell their children of the greatness of His plan, they will live in the shadow of how enormous it is. They will also live in the shadow of how enormous GOD is. It will be a humbling life to know that GOD has chosen him/her for His great purposes.

Pray For That

Our understanding of destiny should prompt us parents to pray. What an awesome responsibility we carry, to raise children whom GOD has chosen to change the world! Where will we find the wisdom to instruct them? We will find ourselves utterly dependent on GOD to work through our lives to at least not mess it up and at best to be actual players in the deal.

We pray knowing that our adversary stands ready to hinder or even destroy the destiny of GOD for them. Prayer is the most powerful weapon we wield against him and we shall not be defeated. Much is at stake when we consider the life of a child. Our children face a formidable opponent and apart from prayer, they have no hope of facing and defeating him.

Pray with them for destiny. One way we communicate calling and purpose is by praying those prayers with our kids. They need to hear mom and dad praying for His destiny in their lives. They pick up on this understanding when they hear this almost every day. I remember hearing Andy Stanley talk about how he prayed with his children regularly that they would have "wisdom to know the right thing to do and courage to do it." He said that before long, they were praying this prayer for themselves. When our children hear us praying for GOD'S destiny in their lives, they too will begin to pray for that and to pursue it as well.

Invite Them to Their Heart

This book has been about the challenges I faced internally. It would have made a world of difference to me as a young man for someone to occasionally tap me on the chest and ask, "Hey, what's going on in there?" Every child needs someone they trust to do just that –

invite them to their heart. Self-understanding is a critical issue for everyone. Until you know who you are, you can only offer the superficial. You cannot offer the depths of your character until you have discovered what lies within. The grasp of GOD'S destiny can only be realized when a person discovers who they are. Otherwise, they simply offer their false-selves to the world.

Teach your children to identify their feelings, the positives and the negatives. Ask them the "why" questions in terms of their motivations and reactions. When they can answer the "why" questions, then they will be able to answer the "who" question. They will begin to discover who they are as they realize why they do what they do. The "why" questions will show them two very important places: 1) places where they need to grow and 2) places where they are gifted. This self-awareness will be a platform from which they can launch into the wide expanse of GOD'S future. You as a parent will be a vital part of that process.

Once a child discovers his heart and knows who he is and what he is all about, this discovery will open up a world of opportunities. Inside of his heart is the DNA that GOD created when this child was being formed in his mother's womb. The desires, dreams and strengths come together in an uncovered heart that points that child in the right direction. Like an arrow propelled from the bow, he will fly straight to the target. He will do so with confidence and excitement. He will become what GOD made him to become and he will do what GOD made him to do.

Show Them Your Heart

Authenticity cannot be taught. It can only be modeled. Our children know us best. They see and experience the best and worst of parents. Our attempts to cover up or wear masks are futile at home. Our families know our failures and they only wait for us to own up to them. If you have not taken the time to travel the road to self-awareness, now is a good time to start. Ask GOD to help you see your own heart. It will be very difficult. However, the results will be so much greater than the hurt you may experience. The healing that comes will bring the wholeness you have desired.

Masks become walls. When our children see us pretending to be people we are not, it creates a huge barrier for them. They begin to question if they can trust us. So they may back away and end up isolated with no one to help them navigate the waters of growing up. They need to know their names. That revelation only happens in a safe place like home.

Should we tell our children about all of our failures? Obviously not. But there will come a time in their lives when they need to know that their father has made bad choices and that their father understands what it is like to fail and to suffer the consequences of those choices. In the moment of discipline, they will feel grace. Instead of isolation, they will feel connected. They will know home is a safe place. No masks are needed.

As you show your children your heart, you will model authenticity for them. It will free them up to do the same. They will be able to live from the depths of their own heart rather than from the shallows of a false-self. They will be able to pursue the destiny for which GOD made them and to which GOD has called them. Perhaps the sun will rise one morning for them when they will have the chance to stand on a mountaintop and look back over their lives. They will see the world is a different place because of them. They will see the legacy they left behind. The ripples of their lives will go far and wide and they will remember a mom and a dad who lived with the desire to see them experience destiny. I know that is my dream for my sons. I am grateful for the journey, where it has taken me and where it is going. I know that I am living GOD'S destiny for my life. It truly has become immeasurably more than all I ask or imagine.

Discussion Questions

1. In Deuteronomy 6:20, Moses said that their children may ask them about why they live like they do. Their answer was to be the story of their salvation, of how GOD supernaturally intervened and rescued them from slavery. Have you ever told your children of GOD'S supernatural intervention in your life?

2. Do you hesitate to tell your children about your journey of faith? Why?

3. What do you believe about the destiny of your children individually?

How are you a part of setting them up to succeed and to fulfill their destiny?

4. How can you as a mom or dad model "living from your heart" for your children?

Survival Tips

This difficult season of waiting was more than helpless waiting. I found that I could be proactive and do some practical things rather than just sit idle. Some of these actions had to do with attitudes while others were physical activities. These are the things I did that enabled me to survive and eventually to thrive.

1. Accept things as they are. Don't try to fight against things or people you cannot change. Here's the reality: If you cannot change them, then you cannot change them. If you can change things, then change things. I tried making things change. I could not do it. Every road I turned was a cul-de-sac. Just go with the flow. It is a tiring time already when you are waiting. The energy you exert trying to change the unchangeable is a waste. You need all the energy you can save during such a season in life. Change what you can and accept what you cannot change. You've heard it prayed in the famous Prayer of Serenity that reads,

> *"Lord, grant me the serenity to accept the things I cannot change, courage to change the things I can and wisdom to know the difference."*

Go with the flow.

2. Believe that GOD is doing something. The season you endure is not a waste of time though it will seem to be just that. There were days we thought that we were wasting time. We knew of places we wanted to go and things we wanted to do. However, we were stuck because we could not change things as they were. It took a long time for us to realize that something positive and productive was happening. It was a radical transformation in our faith to trust GOD when nothing was happening. The silence and stillness was just too much. However, in the process of waiting, we learned to awaken each day with the faith that GOD was accomplishing something significant.

3. It's an inside job. The work GOD is accomplishing are the changes He is creating in your life rather than around your life. I kept looking for Him to change my circumstances. I was praying for a new job and a new location. Fortunately, He said no. He had bigger plans for me than I could even ask. It was a learning experience to realize that when my surroundings were not changing, I was. Once I understood this reality, I could partner with Him. I learned who I was. I began to ask myself questions like: In what areas do I need to grow? How do I need to change? What are the fears I face? What are my strengths? How had my pattern of thinking been a self-defeating process? What was I not seeing about myself? It was such a powerful, revealing work.

4. Maintain some sort of discipline in order to keep your body and mind alert. It was during this season of waiting that I began to take exercise more seriously. For me it was running. For others it may be walking, biking, hiking or racquetball. Just find something you enjoy doing that requires physical movement and then do it. Get moving. Do not sit around. Turn off the television. Stillness will only contribute to your discouragement and it will lead you to deeper places of depression. Also, I read regularly. It was not just Christian books. I read books outside my normal reading routines. I kept expanding my knowledge of things. I wanted this season of waiting to be a growing season. I could not move, but

I could grow. That was something that I could control. Some of the books that were encouraging to me during this season were:

> *The Upside of Adversity*, Os Hillman
> (also received his daily email devotional)
> *Shattered* Dreams, Larry Crabb
> *Kingdom Journeys*, Seth Barnes

Pray and read scripture regularly. Even when there is nothing on the other side of the conversation coming back at you, keep reading and keep praying. GOD is listening. His silence is not His rejection. His silence is your trial. You may not feel like doing any of this, but this is where the discipline comes in. You do these things just like you brush your teeth each morning. It is not a matter of if, but a matter of when. Put these things in your calendar and do not bypass them. Do not allow your emotions to determine your actions. Just do it.

5. Be generous. The temptation when life is hard is to become self-focused. Everything becomes about you. Thinking about others usually is the last thought on your mind. You are just trying to survive and you cannot understand why life is so difficult. To consider the needs of others is a great challenge. One of the ways you keep from becoming self-absorbed and hosting a pity party is by giving yourself away. Find ways to donate money, time and energy to others. Volunteer at organizations. Invest yourself in individuals. When you are generous, it reminds you that you have something to offer to others even when you do not think you do. People need you even when you do not think you matter much. Generous living gets your mind off of yourself. Play your "Yes I can do that" card regularly.

6. Laugh. Even in the midst of sadness, there can be moments of joy. My son said that he cannot remember a day in our house when he did not hear laughter. There are too many videos on the internet not to find something that causes you to laugh. I have kept a file in my desk labeled "comics" for many years. On those days when things were hard, I pulled it out and found something that was humorous. While a moment of laughter does not change things, it does give a minute of relief from the mountain you are climbing. Maintain a sense of humor. Create and look for moments of joy every day. Smile and show the hope within. While that seems to be advice to fake your sadness, it is not. While I worked at hospice, I maintained a sense of joy because of so many, many reasons. Though I was not happy, I did have joy. I was joyous because I was loved deeply by my wife, my children and friends. I was loved by GOD. He had given His Son for me and He would do in a heartbeat for me again if necessary. I had innumerable blessings every day such as food to eat, clothes to wear and a car to drive. Do you know how many people in the world have none of those things? Millions. I had all of those things and they were just the tip of the iceberg. I had good health. I was working with patients who were dying of cancer and heart disease. They struggled to breathe. They could not get out of a bed. They had only a few days left on earth. I was going home after work to run several miles. I may not have all I wanted, but how can a person not smile who has all that I had? I knew that I was greatly blessed and I did not forget it. That gave me joy.

7. Express your emotions. Don't bottle them up. Your emotions need an outlet. You cannot hold them in. If you do, they will explode. Allow tears to flow whether it is from sadness, disappointment or pain. Perhaps you need to give yourself a time limit each day to let your sadness overwhelm you and feel deeply what you are feeling. Then afterwards, dry your eyes, wipe your face and move on with your day. I remember hearing a lady tell how she handled the first Christmas after the death of her adult son. She said that she got up earlier than everyone else, poured herself a cup of coffee, and sat down in the kitchen and cried by herself. After about 30 minutes, she got up, took a shower and enjoyed the rest of the day. Yes you can schedule your sad moments. Talk about your feelings with someone you trust. Tell a loyal friend about your fears and sadness or journal your thoughts. Draw or paint your emotions. Find whatever method works best for you and express regularly what is happening inside.

8. Be kind to yourself. The dark times can be moments when we want to blame ourselves. Negative thoughts are usually pointed inwardly. If you have done something wrong, then admit it and deal with the consequences. If you hurt someone, tell her. Ask for forgiveness. Admit your failure. Restore what needs to be restored. Then move on. Forgive yourself. If you need to forgive yourself each day, then do so. When those feelings of guilt or shame attack your soul, say to yourself, "That's over. I am finished with that. I am forgiven" and then intentionally turn your mind to other things. Awaken each morning with a fresh start in your thoughts. What happened in the past cannot be changed. The future is the only direction that you can control. Walk that way. I have heard people say, "Well if I had known . . . " My response to this idea was to point out the reality, which was simply this: They did not know. How can they hold themselves accountable for something they did not know? Would they hold anyone else in that situation accountable? Absolutely not. You cannot be responsible for what you do not know. If you had known to do something different, you would have done it. Be kind to yourself when life is hard.

9. Keep your flag of hope flying at full mast each day. This darkness is just for a season. It too shall pass although it may not seem like it. For me, this season seemed to last forever. But it did not. Slowly it turned around as I grew and changed. Your season has a final day as well. How do I know? It is because all of them do. Every difficult time in life is always temporary. Even if you are grieving the loss of a loved one, it is temporary. Your heartache may last a long time, perhaps the rest of your life. Still there is coming a day when you can be reunited with your loved one through Jesus Christ. That is the good news of Christ. He conquered death, which means our grief is just for a season. The eternity we spend with them is far, far greater than the grief we will feel without them. While you will have days when your hope is fading like the sun and you are tempted to drop the flag to half-mast, look up. Beyond the sunset is the coming of a new day. Keep your eyes on the horizon.

10. Trust your vision to GOD'S hands. When you have a vision for your life, you learn to know that GOD'S timing is perfect. In the words of Catherine Marshall, *"GOD does have His 'fullness of time for the answer to each prayer."* We cannot understand the depths of GOD'S wisdom and providence, especially when it seems that His schedule is lagging behind our needs. We must trust Him to accomplish the vision He has birthed in us.

These words gave me great hope:

"GOD proves to be good to the man who passionately waits, to the woman who diligently seeks. It's a good thing to quietly hope, quietly hope for help from GOD."
Lamentations 3:25-27, Message

Those who wait upon GOD get fresh strength. They spread their wings and soar like eagles, They run and don't get tired, they walk and don't lag behind.
Isaiah 40:31, Message

Wait for the Lord; be strong and take heart and wait for the Lord. Psalm 27:14

Since ancient times no one has heard, no ear has perceived, no eye has seen any GOD besides you, who acts on behalf of those who wait for him. Isaiah 64:4

Discussion Questions

1. Which of the survival tips resonate most with you? Why?

2. What other tips would you share with someone that has helped you survive a time of waiting on GOD?

"Liminal Space"

Most of us are not very good at waiting in everyday life
or in our spiritual lives. We want what we want and we
want it yesterday.
We want it on our own terms, just like we envisioned it.
When we have to wait in line like everyone else, we are
humbled. When there is something we need, having to
wait for it puts us in a position where we are not in
control. The doctor will see us when s/he is ready. The
cashier will serve us when it is our turn. If we refuse to
wait and abort the process prematurely, we are left
empty-handed.

Richard Rohr calls seasons of waiting "liminal space."
This comes from the Latin word limina which means
threshold. Liminal space is "a unique spiritual position
where human beings hate to be but where the biblical
God is always leading them. It is when you have left the
tried and true, but have not yet been able to replace it
with anything else. It is when you are finally out of the
way. It is when you are between your old comfort zone
and
any possible new answer. If you are not trained in how
to hold anxiety, how to live with ambiguity, how to
entrust and wait, you will run…anything to flee this
terrible cloud of unknowing."
- Ruth Haley Barton[xxv]

Going Where I Had Never Gone Before

"Come to the edge."
"We can't. We are afraid."
"Come to the edge."
"We can't. We will fall!"

"Come to the edge."
And they came. And he pushed them.
And they flew.

- Christopher Logue[xxvi]

I finally did it. I finally completed a marathon run – 26.2 miles. It took me more than two years to finally get there, but I did. In case you are wondering, it was not a sanctioned race. In fact, it was my own. I called it "The Bruce Pittman Pro/Am Invitational I Will Finish This If I Have to Crawl" Marathon. No tee shirts were given out. No medals were awarded. The main goal was to finish. And I did. I finished.

As I looked back, I realized that my marathon training was a perfect picture of this season of my life. Prior to this time in life, I had occasionally run as a regular exercise routine. However I had never entertained the idea of running a marathon. In fact, several years earlier, I had run in several 5K runs (3.1 miles) when a friend came up to me and said, "I did not know you were a marathoner." I laughed and quickly replied, "I'm not. I am just running 5K runs." I could not even fathom running 26.2 miles then. I thought that distance was ridiculous. It was too much for me to imagine. But I began running further and as I did, 26.2

miles was no longer overwhelming. I could see it happening in my mind and as I did, I began to run further and further. Each time, I would think to myself, "I've never run this far before." Those runs were new territory for me. I was going where I had never gone before.

Making Me Stronger

That was my experience during this time of disorientation. GOD took me places I had never gone before and I was persevering in ways I had never imagined. I remember numerous occasions when during the summer months I would think, "There is no way we can be in this same situation by Christmas." Christmas would come and there we would be – in the same situation. It happened over and over and over. It was like an unending marathon. I would hope to see a finish line, but it was always a mirage. I kept trudging along, one foot in front of the other.

I remember one specific summer afternoon run on a two-lane country road that was not normally busy. It had a few curves in it so I was especially cautious about running on the shoulder rather than the road itself to ensure that drivers would not be surprised by a runner. On this particular day, it was very hot. I was near the end of my run and I was tired. In the middle of the one of those curves came an unusual line of cars streaming by me in both directions at a high rate of speed. The shoulder had numerous fire ant beds that were forcing me to use the avoidance technique of skipping and hopping in order not to step on them. In the back of my mind was the frightening thought of stepping on a rattlesnake. In my exhaustion I prayed, "GOD are You trying to kill me here? I need some relief." As I prayed those words, I realized that was exactly how I felt about our circumstances at that time, like GOD had left us on the side of the road to fend for ourselves. His response in my thoughts was, "Why do you want things easy? I am developing in you a strong mind and a strong heart. I am enabling you to persevere." I continued running and safely arrived at home that day. I also continued running spiritually and I was getting stronger. It did not make life any easier, but at least it helped to begin answering the question of why I was going through this time.

Eyes on Jesus

On numerous occasions during this season of life, the book of Hebrews was great encouragement to me. In Hebrews 12 (Message paraphrase), the writer reminded me of how even Jesus had to persevere in order to finish well. Jesus did not have it easy. The one guy who could raise the dead died. How can that even happen? That is ridiculous. But it happened. Jesus had to sweat it out.

Keep your eyes on Jesus, who both began and finished this race we're in. Study how he did it. Because he never lost sight of where he was headed—that exhilarating finish in and with God—he could put up with anything along the way: Cross, shame, whatever. And now he's there,
in the place of honor, right alongside God. When you find yourselves flagging in your faith, go over that story again, item by item, that long litany of hostility he plowed through.
That will shoot adrenaline into your souls!

And then he reminded me of why GOD was allowing this season of my life. It was His love.

God is educating you; that's why you must never drop out. He's treating
you as dear children. This trouble you're in isn't punishment; it's training, the normal experience of children. Only irresponsible parents leave children to fend for themselves. Would you prefer an irresponsible God? We respect our own parents for training and not spoiling us, so why not embrace God's training so we can truly live? While we were children, our parents did what seemed best to them. But God is doing what is best for us, training us to live God's holy best.
At the time, discipline isn't much fun. It always feels like it's going against the grain. Later, of course, it pays off handsomely, for it's the well-trained who find themselves mature in their relationship with God.

I was becoming mature in my relationship with GOD. My heavenly Father was allowing or creating my circumstances that were training me because of His love for me, His son. And yet prior to this season of life, I thought that I was mature. Little did I realize how immature I was. My faith was shallow and weak and childish. GOD was developing in me a faith that was strong and resilient and mature. I did not even know it. My self-awareness was growing. I was learning who I was through these tough times. And GOD was making me more than I ever could imagine. He was taking me places I had never gone before. A new life was opening up before me.

Mental Toughness

My greatest challenge was mental. I had to develop mental toughness to overcome the obstacles I faced internally. The biggest hurdle was my own mind. I remember one particular trail run I participated in. It was called the Cheetah Chase. Fortunately there was no cheetah chasing us. It was an eight-mile meandering run through a forest. As I came to the six-mile marker, I noticed a guy in a red shirt ahead of me. Since the trail had numerous curves in it, I could not tell how far ahead of me he was, but I kept catching a glimpse of him through the trees to my right or my left. We came to a clearing and I saw him ahead of me and I thought, "Hey I can catch him." But I was tired after six miles of running. I debated it for a few more yards and then I made my decision. I set my eyes on him and quickened my pace. I caught him about a half mile from the finish. After passing him, I realized, "Oh, now I must keep ahead of him. I can't let him pass me." So I kept up my pace and 100 yards from the finish line, I could feel him coming up on me. If you've never run, then this does not make sense to you, but you do not hear people catching you, you feel them catching you. I could feel him on my heels so I had to kick it to a faster pace in order to beat him. Please understand that neither one of us was running for first or second or third or any honorable place. We were racing each other so I had to beat him. I had no other option. I shifted to another gear and when we passed the finish line, I was ahead of him by no more than a half step. But I finished and I won (well, I beat the guy in the red shirt). Just when I thought I could run no faster and no farther, I did. It was all mental. I had the physical ability to do it, but I did not have the mental tenacity to do it. GOD changed all of that. I was learning to finish and to finish well.

Tell Another Story

Tony Robbins is a well-known motivational speaker. I do not agree with all of his ideas, but one story I read made a lot of sense to me. It is told by Asha Hawkesworth.[xxvii]

During one of Tony's seminars, a woman was trying to explain, in excruciating detail, what was wrong in her life. He let her talk for a while and then he said to her, "Tell another story." She began her sad story again and why she could not go forward. Tony repeated, "Tell another story." But like a broken record, she kept going. In order to get her attention, Tony began to bark like a dog literally. It was the only way to get her to stop. The more he told her to tell another story, the more determined she became to tell the one that she was used to telling. When she finally stopped, he repeated, "Tell another story."

GOD was not only taking me to new places during this season of lostness, He was turning the page and beginning to write a new chapter in the story of my life. Early on in this adventure, I recorded these words in my journal:

"I've realized that though I've grown deeper in the things of GOD, I have only scratched the surface. There are higher heights, deeper depths and more expansive places where GOD desires to take me. The journey has just begun."

Little did I know how true those words were. My past would not always define me. While it was a part of my story, it would not be the whole story. GOD had a future for me and He was preparing me for it. He was taking me there because He redeems all things, especially the broken places. From our story of brokenness and lostness, He creates a new story of healing and redemption. From ashes comes beauty. From death comes life.

The words of Jeremiah 29:11 (The Message) have given me confidence in the future. To the exiled Jews, Jeremiah was inspired to write:

This is God's Word on the subject: "As soon as Babylon's seventy years are up and not a day before, I'll show up and take care of you as I promised and bring you back home.
I know what I'm doing. I have it all planned out—plans to take care of you, not abandon you, plans to give you the future you hope for.

While their past involved an exile because of their sin, that was not the whole story. There was more waiting for them. GOD would take them there. He was preparing them for it.

The knowledge that GOD had it all planned inspired me during those moments when fear and negativity were sitting on my shoulders whispering in my ears. GOD was working His plan perfectly, and He still is. I have battles to fight, ground to gain and victories to secure. I am looking forward to all that GOD has in store for me. This journey has awakened me to the truly great adventure of following Jesus. It was something I had only read about, but now it has become a part of my story, a story I can now tell.

Begin Today; Write a New Story

The same is true for you, too. Though your previous marriage failed, your present marriage does not need to fail. Though you lost a job, you do not always have to be unemployed. While those seasons made you who are now, they also prepared you to write another story. Your past regrets and disappointments do not always have to define you. You can write a new story beginning today.

Perhaps you are uncertain about telling your story. But I can tell you that someone needs your story. Someone is enduring a painful trial right now that you have already survived. It may be divorce or cancer or miscarriage. You know the heaviness and loneliness of it all. They need to know that you survived. They need to know that faith in GOD is more than a theory. They need to know that their feelings are normal. They need to know that someone really does understand and that someone truly cares. You are that person. Your story is the connection.

Pick up the pen and write. Tell your story of transformation and hope and healing. Tell about the moment when you became more than you were. It will be legendary, a story of battles you fought, journeys you traveled and enemies you conquered. It has victory written all over it. For that is the heart of our strong and passionate GOD – to make you more than a conqueror.

Discussion Questions

1. What is the most dangerous chance you have ever taken (like bungee jumping)?

2. What dangerous new places has GOD taken you?
Did you want to go there? What skills did you gain – like flying?

3. Did you discover who you were? Are you telling a new story?

Who needs to hear this story?

About the Author

Bruce Pittman has served as a pastor of churches in Georgia and North Carolina for more than twenty years. Bruce is a graduate of Mercer University, Southeastern Baptist Seminary and Samford University. He and his wife, Kim, have been married since 1984 and have two adult sons.

End Notes

Chapter 1 – No One Ever Told Me

[i] Thomas Merton was an Anglo-American Catholic writer and mystic. A Trappist monk of the Abbey of Gethsemani, Kentucky, he was a poet, social activist, and student of comparative religion. Merton wrote more than 70 books, mostly on spirituality, social justice and a quiet pacifism.

[ii] *Lent Meditations 2012*, David Loo, Editor, Trinity Annual Conference, Methodist Church in Malaysia, March 8, 2012, page 24.

[iii] Seth Barnes, *Kingdom Journeys* (Ashland, OR: Ashland Press, 2012), 105.

Chapter 2 – GOD Confusing Me

[iv] Lonnie Riley and John Franklin, *Faith - Living in the Certainty of GOD'S Reality* (Nashville, TN: Lifeway Press, 2006), 44.

[v] Os Hillman, *The Upside of Adversity* (Ventura, CA: Regal Books, 2006), 65.

Chapter 3 – Dealing With the Disappointment

[vi] Used by permission. Hall, John Mark and Chapman, Steven Curtis. *"Voice of Truth."* Lyrics. Performed by Casting Crowns. Casting Crowns. Beach Street Records, 2003. See Acknowledgements Page.

Chapter 4 – Radical Re-Do

[vii] As quoted by Seth Barnes, *Kingdom Journeys*, (Ashland, OR: Ashland Press, 2012), 52.

from:
http://www.brainyquote.com/quotes/quotes/e/ellamailla3
25075.html
Ella Maillart was a French-speaking Swiss adventurer,
travel writer and photographer, as well as a
sportswoman.

Chapter 5 – Jesus at the Wheel
[viii] Os Hillman, *The Upside of Adversity* (Ventura, CA:
Regal Books, 2006), 65.

Chapter 6 – A Heart Disconnected
[ix] Henry Cloud and John Townsend, *How People Grow*
(Grand Rapids, MI: Zondervan, 2001), 87.
[x] John Eldredge, *Wild at Heart* (Nashville, TN: Thomas
Nelson Publishers, 2001), 189.

Chapter 7 – A Heart Discovered
[xi] John Eldredge, *Wild at Heart* (Nashville, TN: Thomas
Nelson Publishers, 2001), 149.
[xii] Attributed to Philo, a first-century Jewish philosopher.
[xiii] Jessi's story is found in Seth Barnes, *Kingdom
Journeys* (Ashland, OR: Ashland Press, 2012), 52ff.

Chapter 8 – Running the Race
[xiv] Richard Hendrix, quoted in Leadership Journal,
Volume 7, Number 3.

Chapter 9 – Back Up From the Trees, See the Forest
[xv] John MacDuff, Sermon: "The Promised Land!"
http://www.gracegems.org/2011/08/trust.html

Chapter 10 – GOD'S Wonderful Gifts

[xvi] Jeff Goins, *The In-Between* (Chicago: Moody Publishers, 2013), 157.

[xvii] John Ortberg, "Don't Waste a Crisis", Leadership Journal, Winter 2011,
See:
http://www.christianitytoday.com/le/2011/winter/dontwastecrisis.html

[xviii] Quoted by Leighton Ford, *The Attentive Life* (Multnomah, 2008), p. 162. See:
http://www.preachingtoday.com/illustrations/2008/july/3072108.html

Chapter 12 – What's Your Name?

[xix] Henry Cloud and John Townsend, *GOD Will Make a Way* (Nashville, TN: Integrity Publishers, 2002), 271.

[xx] Carol Kent has lived every parent's nightmare. After her only son was sentenced to life in prison without the possibility of parole, Carol's life took a permanent detour. She and her husband, Gene, have been adjusting ever since, moving to Florida to be near the prison, starting a new ministry for prison inmates and their families, and sharing the faithfulness of God.
http://www.carolkent.org/

Chapter 13 – Leading From a True Heart

[xxi] See: http://www.gloriarose.com/?p=1780. Gloria Rose is a writer, teacher and life coach. She helps people uncover their true gifts and calling and then live it out.

[xxii] See http://www.laraequy.com/blog/   November 11, 2012. Larae was an undercover FBI agent for 25 years. She is author of the book, *Secrets of a Strong Mind*. Presently Larae helps people uncover their own story and overcome the barriers to becoming all that GOD made them to be.

[xxiii] http://www.churchleaders.com/pastors/pastor-how-to/164948-john-holm-well-defined-leader.html. John Holm is a leadership consultant with TAG Consulting. See www.transformingchurch.net

Chapter 14 – The Thing Before Us

[xxiv] http://www.ktul.com/story/16428626/with-depression-helping-others-may-in-turn-help-you
[xxv] As quoted by Ruth Haley Barton (founder of the Transforming Center) in her Advent Series – Leaders in Waiting.
http://www.transformingcenter.org/2012/11/advent-leaders-in-waiting/
Richard Rohr is a Franciscan friar, internationally known inspirational speaker and author. Rohr is the founder of the New Jerusalem Community and the Center for Action and Contemplation.

Chapter 17 – Going Where I Had Never Gone Before

[xxvi] Logue, Christopher. "Come to the Edge." *New Numbers.* London: Cape, 1969. pp. 65-66.
[xxvii] See: http://www.brighthill.net/articles/does_telling_your_story_heal_you_or_hold_you_ back. htm# sth ash.9r9H3unJ.dpbs